F-117 STEALTH

in action

By Jim Goodall
Color By Don Greer
Illustrated by Joe Sewell

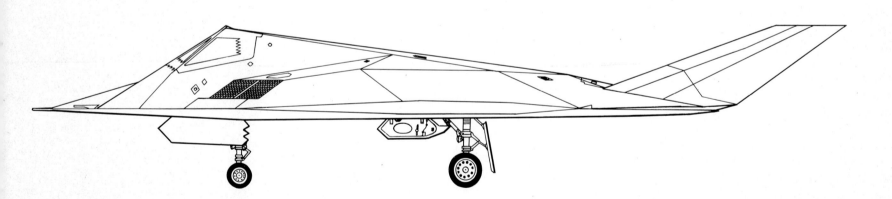

Aircraft Number 115
squadron/signal publications

A pair of F-117As of the 37th Tactical Fighter Wing attack targets in Iraq on the night of 16 January 1991. The wing was led by COL Al Whitley, who had assumed command only a few days before the wing deployed two squadrons of F-117As to Saudi Arabia.

Author's Note

One of the problems in researching military weapons systems is the availability of public information. When you're dealing with a classified program such as the F-117; the task is even more difficult. Rumors surfaced about a Lockheed Stealth program during mid-1977. John Andrews (of Testors Corporation) and I heard that something was flying in Nevada with the name *Have Blue*, which was the code name for the Stealth prototype.

On 5 May 1978, a Las Vegas paper reported the loss of a secret aircraft flown by Lockheed Test Pilot, Bill Park. All that was said was that the aircraft had a problem, he ejected and was severely injured. With that news article, I started digging and since it was a Lockheed program, I knew it was Black; that is, highly classified.

During the 1970s and early 1980s, pieces of information kept surfacing. A lot was accurate, but it was like a blind man describing an elephant. The parts were right, but not in the correct order. A former Lockheed pilot stated he saw a drawing which looked like a Douglas F4D Skyray with Packard grills for air intakes.

I have spent a total of fifteen days at the northern fence line of the Tonopah Test Range Facility. Some of the first photographs of the F-117 to appear in print were either mine or my good friend, Tony Landis, and we have both enjoyed a lot of attention by having the first photos of the Stealth.

Millions of people have had the opportunity to view the F-117 since its 21 April 1990 public debut and it has been the star attraction at dozens of airshows; although the pilots never talk about its capability. They will say, "It is an all Black single seat aircraft, powered by twin General Electric engines. It was built by Lockheed and is flown by the 37th TFW at Tonopah, Nevada. There were fifty-nine built." That is as far as they'll go; any other questions get an, "I'm sorry, its classified" or "No comment." This book will hopefully answer some of the questions on the F-117.

Dedication:

In memory of two F-117A pilots who lost their lives in service to their country: MAJ Ross E. Mulhare, USAF and MAJ Michael C. Stewart, USAF, both of the 4450th TG.

Acknowledgements:

There are hundreds of people that I should thank, but that would take some forty or fifty pages. The following people deserve special thanks. First and foremost this book is a reality because of the organization headed by (now retired) Ben R. Rich, President of Lockheed Skunk Works from 1975 until 17 January 1991. Second, my right hand during the writing of this book, Debilee Anderson of Minneapolis; I thank her with all my heart. And to Terry and Carol Love, who's kindness and friendship was like a port in a very bad storm.

Photo Credits

Shelley J. Goodall
John Andrews, Testors Corp
Joel Putman
Robert Arance
Kevin Patrick
Mick Roth
COL Sconyers, HQ/TAC/PA
Eric Schulzinger, Lockheed
General Electric
COL Tony Tolin, 37th TFW/CC
John Lear
Tom Rosquin, Thomas Aviation
Pete Eames, Security/Special Projects
Bill Sweetman - Janes
Miss Edwards, 57th FWW/PA
COL Knox Bishop
Alan Welch

Terry Love
Jay Miller, Aerofax
Nick Benfatto
Chuck Mayer
James Eastman
James P. Stevenson
LTC Weber, HQ/TAC/PA
Richard Stadler
COL Ken Dyson, USAF Ret.
TSGT Bobby Sheldon, 37th TFW/PA
Mike Dornheim, Aviation Week
Tony Landis
Ben R. Rich, Lockheed ADP
Bill Park, Lockheed
Jim Mesko
MAJ Greg Kreis, 57th FWW/PAO

An F-117A flies over the Salton Sea near Palm Springs, California. The aircraft has its UHF communication antenna extended and is carrying a removable anti-collision beacon on the port side of the upper fuselage. (Eric Schulzinger)

Introduction

The Lockheed Advanced Development Projects (ADP), better known by its nickname — the Skunk Works, has over the years built an aerospace design team capable of achieving what can truly be called incredible feats of aircraft design and development.

When Kelly Johnson first conceived the U-2, nobody thought that it was possible to build a jet powered glider that could reach and maintain 80,000 feet. When the original Blackbird (the A-12/YF-12/SR-71) was conceived during 1958/59, an aircraft that could fly at Mach 3.2 at or above 90,000 feet was totally unheard of.

One of the major problem areas faced by the Air Force during Viet Nam was the loss of a large number of aircraft to radar-guided guns and surface-to-air missiles. One way to reduce these losses was to reduce the radar cross section of the attack aircraft itself. Current designs did not allow stealth technology to be applied, with the exception of the B-1 bomber. The B-1A had a radar cross section (RCS) of approximately 10 square meters; the B-1B has a radar cross section of approximately 1 square meter. That reduction primarily dealt with the air intakes and other external features on the aircraft.

Stealth technology was identified as one potential solution to the problems associated with a high threat environment. If the radar cross section (RCS) of the aircraft could be reduced dramatically, the performance and capability of all radar-guided defensive systems would be degraded. In other words, the Soviet Union's two hundred billion dollar air defense system would become useless.

Stealth technology had been developed in many experimental programs, most of them classified, since the late 1940s. Lockheed has been dealing with low observables in operational aircraft since the late 1950s. The most notable success in this field was the A-12/YF-12/SR-71. The SR-71 is 107 feet long, 56 feet wide and cruises at speeds above Mach 3. But what is really amazing is that this was the first generation production Stealth type aircraft. The Blackbird has a radar cross section of some 22 square inches making it a relatively small radar target. This, along with its speed and altitude capabilities, is the Blackbird's main defense against interception.

During 1975 Skunk Works engineers began working on a computerized program that would allow reduced radar cross section techniques to be coupled with aerodynamics to come up with a flyable aircraft design. One of the technologies that evolved was a process known as faceting, a design process by which the aircraft surface radiates 99.9% of the reflected radar energy from a radar source away from its receiver. If they could produce such a surface and still allow the airplane to fly aerodynamically, they would have a true low observable aircraft.

A number of companies were studying Stealth technology, including Northrop, Boeing, and General Dynamics. They all realized that the process of faceting, building an airplane with physical characteristics that would reduce the radar cross section, offered the best chance to produce a workable Stealth aircraft in the shortest possible time and make it operational.

In early 1977, Lockheed received a contract from the Defense Advanced Research Projects Agency, better known as DARPA, to build and test two subscale (about 60% of the size of an operational aircraft) Stealth Strike Fighters, using faceting, under the code name *Have Blue*.

This Lockheed/CIA A-12 on the ramp at Groom dry lake is parked in front of the hangars that housed the *Have Blue* and early F-117As. The A-12 was a first generation "Stealthy" aircraft.

Have Blue

Shortly after the contract was let, the DARPA *Have Blue* program was transferred to Air Force control and became a "Black" (highly classified/compartmentalized) program. As of early 1991, the *Have Blue* program was still so classified that even people within the Skunk Works who have access to the F-117 program had no access to the *Have Blue* project.

There were two aircraft built and both were destroyed in accidents. Reportedly, there are photos of the aircraft, but they are highly classified and according to Pete Eames (USAF security manager), they will never be released to the public. The criteria for declassification of information under his control is, "a program will be declassified if there is a direct benefit of declassification to the United States Government and for no other reason."

The *Have Blue* prototypes were manufactured at Lockheed's Burbank, California facility in just a matter of months. Lockheed built the two aircraft using a large number of off-the-shelf components: General Electric J85 engines, A-10 landing gear for the main gear and fly-by-wire components from the F-16. This allowed Lockheed to build two prototypes in record time and under budget (37 million dollars for both aircraft). The prototypes were disassembled, and shipped to the Groom Lake Test Facility for testing. Because of a strike at Lockheed, management and supervisory personnel reassembled the *Have Blue* aircraft.

Lockheed test pilot Bill Park made the first flight in either January or February of 1978 from the DOD secret test facility at Groom Lake, Nevada. The second aircraft joined the program in March or April of that same year. Park was being assisted in flight tests by United States Air Force LTC Ken Dyson (later chief test pilot for the Northrop B-2).

The shape of the *Have Blue* prototype is classified, although it is believed to generally resemble the F-117, except that the twin rudders were located forward of the exhaust ejectors and angled inward. The wing trailing was less deeply notched than the F-117A, there was no weapons bay and the nose probes were absent.

On 4 May 1978, Bill Park was landing after a routine test flight with the first prototype when a high-sink-rate problem arose. The aircraft hit the ground hard, jamming the right main landing gear in a semi-retracted position. Bill brought the aircraft down hard on its left main gear three times, trying to shake the gear loose. It didn't work and he was told to climb to 10,000 feet, burn off fuel and eject. The force of the ejection knocked Bill's head against the headrest, knocking him unconscious, and he was still unconscious when he hit the ground.

Shortly after he ejected, the aircraft ran out of fuel. It came down like a falling leaf, wobbled around, lost control, went inverted, and went straight in. Bill Park survived the crash, but because of his injuries, he was removed from flight status and never flew again. He retired as Lockheed's Director of Flight Operations during September of 1989 and never had an opportunity to fly the F-117.

From mid-1978 until early 1980, Ken Dyson flew the remainder of the test missions with the second *Have Blue* aircraft. He flew more than sixty-five sorties, many of them against threat radars. These tests revealed the importance of RCS reduction. Door and access panels were sealed before each series of flights with metallic tape, which compensated for differences in conductivity between different parts of the skin. RAM (Radar Absorbent Material) was then applied over the gap.

A paint type RAM was available, but it had to be built up coat by coat by hand. To cover the large areas, RAM came in flexible sheets very similar to linoleum. It had to be cut to shape and bonded to the skin. Landing gear doors and all other access panels had to be adjusted for fit between flights and even the gaps around the canopy and the fuel filler door had to be filled with paint-type RAM before each radar signature test.

The attention to detail required for this design had to be extended to the design of the leading edges of all access panels, as well as the type of screws used on the panels (conventional slot headed screws showed up like a barn door on the radar range: a series of ten screws lined in a row could increase the RCS by a factor of 1,000).

On one of the flights, the *Have Blue* aircraft bloomed, or showed up, dramatically on radar at a much greater range than ever before. An inspection after the aircraft landed revealed that three screws were not quite tight and were extended above the skin. They were retightened and the test was repeated successfully.

The *Have Blue* aircraft was essentially undetectable by any airborne radar in the world except the Boeing E-3 AWACS, which only acquired the aircraft at very short ranges. Most ground based missile tracking radars could not detect it until it was well inside the missile's minimum range. Additionally, the missile onboard guidance radars could not lock on to the aircraft. This also held true for air-to-air radar-guided missiles.

The test results of the *Have Blue* program led William Perry, Defense Under-Secretary for Research and Engineering, to urge the Air Force to apply Stealth technology to an operational aircraft. During 1980, Defense Secretary Harold Brown stated that the Carter Administration had increased spending on Stealth by a factor of 100. The majority of this increase went into the development and production of a full-size, operational Lockheed Stealth Strike Aircraft under the code name *Senior Trend*, with the designation F-117A.

It was realized that the F-117A development program would need a secure location for testing and later operational flights. It could no longer be kept at Groom Lake, which is primarily used for testing of classified programs. On the other hand, the program was so sensitive that it could not be assigned to a conventional Air Force base, so a new base had to be built.

The site selected was the former Sandia Labs nuclear weapons aerodynamic test facility (basically a runway and a hangar) located approximately forty miles southeast of Tonopah, Nevada, on the northern edge of the Nellis Air Force Base test range. Construction began during 1980 and it was completed in two phases.

The base was named the Tonopah Test Range (better known as the TTR) and consists of a 12,000 foot runway and fifty-four individual hangars. Six additional identical hangars arranged in two groups of three are utilized for aircraft maintenance, avionics maintenance, and systems support. There are also two large hangars at the south end of the ramp which were originally used to house the Soviet built aircraft flown by the Red Hats (4477th Test and Evaluation Squadron).

The Air Force decided to build the TTR because there was no room at the Groom Lake Test Facility and the proximity to the Nellis complex was also considered very important. Since the Nellis complex is roughly the size of Switzerland, the aircraft would have plenty of room to operate unobserved. The site was not quite perfect from a security view point because the runway was overlooked by public land. On the other hand, it was not a place likely to draw a casual visitor. As someone who has been to the northern fence line of the TTR on six different occasions, I can attest that the base is in the middle of absolutely nowhere.

The aircraft operating out of Tonopah are serviced primarily at the TTR with the major periodic depot maintenance, or PDM, being performed at the Lockheed facility, Plant 10 (Air Force Plant 42), Palmdale, California.

Have Blue

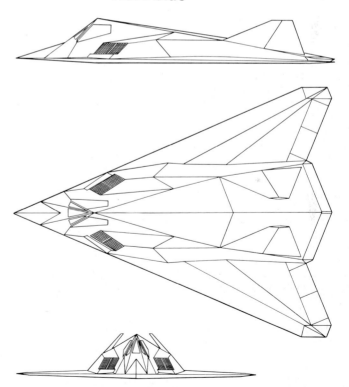

Development

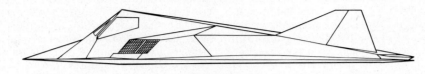

Have Blue

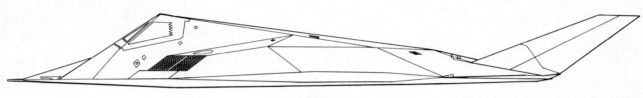

F-117 FSD

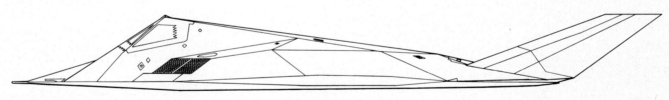

F-117A

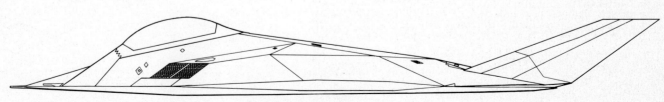

Two Seat Proposal

F-117A

During November of 1978, Congress authorized full scale development of the Lockheed Stealth Strike Fighter under the designation F-117A. The first five aircraft produced were preproduction full scale development aircraft (FSD) which differed from the production F-117A in having a smaller fin and rudder. The first aircraft flew in June of 1981 and after successful testing, an initial production run of twenty aircraft was authorized. Soon after the program was funded, Congress authorized production of a full wing, instead of a squadron. As a result, funding was passed for a total of fifty-nine production aircraft.

The production F-117A is an ugly duckling of an aircraft. It is humpbacked and thick where most aircraft are sleek and tapered. It is made of geometrically flat panels rather than smooth, compound curves. Its sharply swept wings and tail imply high speeds, but the body shape emphatically does not imply high speed.

The F-117A is big — actually larger than an F-15. It weighs about the same as an F-15 (without missiles or external fuel) and, like the F-15, stands high off the ground. It is the aircraft's stealth characteristics that make the F-117A look so strange.

Aircraft designs used to center around aerodynamics, followed by propulsion systems and with electrical systems as a low priority. Stealth aircraft (as designed by Lockheed) reverse the process, being designed according to the principles of electrical engineering. Radar energy generates an electromagnetic (EM) field around the aircraft, making it behave like an antenna. The stealth designer's job was first to design a very bad antenna, then make it fly. This was done through faceting the aircraft's surfaces.

Faceting does not absorb radar energy, but rather eliminates the curved surfaces that radiate radar energy back to the transmitting and receiving source. By faceting the aircraft, you can control the direction that the radiated radar beam will go. The surface of the F-117A has about a half dozen different types of repeated angles on the entire aircraft. This allows the radar energy to be reflected away from the hostile transmitter/receiver. To further lessen reflected radar energy, Lockheed applied RAM (Radar Absorbent Material) material on the aircraft surfaces.

The F-117A reportedly handles well for such a large aircraft. Its landing characteristics are not unlike delta winged aircraft such as the F-102, F-106 and French Mirage. Landing and takeoff speeds are high because of the aircraft's sharply swept wing and a drag parachute is always used on landing.

The aircraft flies nose high at low speeds and decelerates rapidly in sharp turns. The absence of curved surfaces on the aircraft does not appear to affect its flight characteristics in any way. The flight controls are conventional: there are two elevon sections on each wing, twin fins with all moving rudders which have no pitch control function, and a fly-by-wire control system.

The F-117A is inherently unstable and without the quadredundant fly-by-wire flight control system (similar to an F-16) the F-117A would not fly. According to aerodynamic engineers associated with the program, it would be extremely difficult, if not impossible, to design a practical Stealth aircraft with three axis of neutral stability without fly-by-wire. The only part of the F-117A flight control system that is different from its non-Stealth counterparts is the means that the F-117A senses air data. In place of conventional pitch and yaw vanes used on most modern fighters and attack aircraft, the F-117A has four individual static pitot probes on the aircraft nose. Each of the four-sided pitot heads have tiny holes on each facet. Differential readings from each hole provide pitch and yaw information to the flight control system.

This F-117A Stealth fighter (802) was the eighteenth aircraft delivered to the USAF on 6 April 1984. The aircraft flies over the Nevada desert with its lower communication antenna (under the unit insignia on the fuselage) extended. (Eric Schulzinger).

Fin Development

F-117 FSD

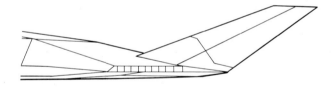

F-117A

Enlarged Fin/Rudder

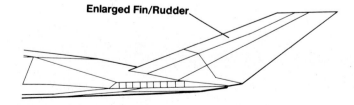

The F-117A is constructed largely of aluminum, with some titanium in the engine and exhaust systems. It has a complex skeletal structure to which the main facets are separately fastened. This is the only way to achieve the required accuracy of the facet leading edges. The exterior skin is covered by radar absorption material which reduces what is left of the radar reflection from the facets. RAM is believed to consist of magnetic iron particles, ferrite particles and polymer binders. It can be applied as a putty-like material or as a paint. RAM type putty is used over the screw heads on the FLIR (the Forward Looking Infrared), DLIR (Downward Looking Infrared) and some of the panels just forward to the windscreen.

Originally, RAM came as flexible sheets in six different types, depending on the area of the aircraft to be covered. It was bonded to a metal matrix wire mesh which was in turn bonded to the airframe of the F-117A. When the aircraft entered service, the Air Force commissioned a new facility in which the aircraft was held in a rotating fixture and RAM material was applied using robotics and computer controlled nozzles.

The F-117A has twin weapons bays under the fuselage on the aircraft centerline. These bays have the same internal weapons capability as the F-111 and typical loads consist of two 2,000 pound smart bombs (such as the BLU 109s, Paveway II and III, the AGM 130) as well as some specially designed weapons built or modified for F-117A use. The bays can carry up to two Mark 61 Tactical Nuclear Weapons. The F-117A does **not** have an assigned nuclear mission; however, all TAC aircraft are designed with the capability to carry nuclear weapons. For long range ferry flights, fuel tanks can be installed in the weapons bays to increase the range.

The F-117A is powered by two 10,800 lbst General Electric F404-F1D2 engines (non-afterburning variants of the F/A-18 engines). Two unique features of the F-117A are the engine air intakes and exhaust systems. Both are designed to mask the signature of the engine. From the front it presents a whirling mass of reflective metal (the turbine blades). From the rear there is a similar mass plus the infrared signature of the exhaust gases.

To reduce the engine radar cross section, the inlet ducts are masked by composite grids covered with RAM. The spaces in the grids are smaller than the wave length of most radars, so they reflect the energy away from the receiver in the same way the aircraft's surface does. Radar energy that does penetrate the grid is absorbed by RAM within the duct.

At low speeds the inlets are augmented by suck-in doors on the fuselage above the inlet ducts. The grids are electrically heated; however, even a small amount of ice can readily cause problems. As a result, there is a light on each side of the cockpit positioned to illuminate the inlets, so the pilot can check them for ice.

The exhaust system ducts the circular engine exhaust section into a narrow slot at the trailing edge of the fuselage. The lower lip of the slot is longer than the upper edge and bends slightly upwards, masking the exhaust completely from below the aircraft. The exhaust plume is the most visible part of the aircraft in the Infrared spectrum. It is wide and flat but cools rapidly a short distance behind the aircraft. The exhaust slot has a row of twelve vertical baffles which help mask the interior from radar and provides structural strength. Without these baffles the exhaust would tend to bulge under pressure. The exhaust system is complex, incorporating sliding elements and quartz tiles to resist heat without changing shape.

Another unique feature of the F-117A is the complex canopy which provides adequate visibility for normal flight conditions. Visibility to the rear and above is restricted. The flat glass panels are treated to reduce radar reflectivity and the entire canopy opens for access to the cockpit. It is a heavy unit and uses explosives to jettison it in case of an ejection. On top of the canopy is a small, low intensity light that illuminates the rotating refueling receptacle.

The cockpit is equipped with a conventional head-up display (HUD) which is more capable than the F-15C, but not as capable as the F-15E. Some pilots felt that the HUD, along with the FLIR CRT, gave more information than they needed to fly the aircraft. The main control panel has two standard five inch multi-function display CRTs, while the main FLIR/DLIR CRT has a twelve inch screen and the aircraft is primarily flown using the FLIR/DLIR CRT display.

The F-117A's unique navigation and attack system is located in front of the cockpit. The aircraft is fitted with a comprehensive electro/optical unit to find and identify targets without betraying its presence. The forward looking infrared (FLIR) sensor is located just below the windscreen and below the leading edge of the canopy. It is covered by a very fine wire mesh grid that is almost identical to the grid over the engine air inlets. Although it is transparent and allows imagery to be seen without the unit being detected,

This F-117A (807) is parked on the north taxiway of the Tonapah Test Range, Nevada. The landing gear and interior of all landing gear well doors are in White. No. 807 was the twenty-third F-117A produced and was delivered on 28 November 1984. (Eric Schulzinger)

The F-117A was the star attraction at the 1990 air show at Carswell AFB, Texas. This was one of the first displays of the Stealth after its unveiling at Nellis AFB and drew an estimated crowd of over one half million. (Alan Welch)

it appears the same as a flat panel to hostile radar.

The FLIR sensor is housed in a steerable turret containing a dual field of view sensor. A second unit is located under the fuselage on the starboard side of the nosewheel well. This bay houses the downward looking infrared (DLIR) sensor. Both sensor turrets contain a bore sighted laser for illuminating the target for laser-guided weapons. These sensors are backed up by a highly accurate internal navigation system (INS) that uses an electrostatic suspended gyro.

The INS guides the aircraft to the approximate target area and points the FLIR's wide field of view lens toward the target (when the FLIR is not being used it is rotated 180 degrees to keep debris from damaging the sensor). When the F-117A approaches the target (or a turn point), the pilot monitors the target on the FLIR/DLIR. When the specific target is located, the pilot selects the narrow field of view, confirms identification, selects the aim point and locks on. As the target disappears underneath the F-117A, the DLIR acquires and continues to track the target. The DLIR laser illuminates the target approximately 7 to 10 seconds before impact allowing the weapon to be guided accurately (DOD released FLIR video tapes taken over Baghdad showed that the F-117A has the ability to hit a 1 meter target from 25,000 feet, at night).

All operational F-117As are single seat aircraft. There was a proposal for an elevated cockpit two seater trainer, which was to use the wreckage of the first production aircraft. Since the F-117A flies so well, however, it was felt that there was no need for a trainer.

The thin exhaust ejector system blends cool air with the engine exhaust to lower the aircraft's infrared signature. Additionally, the extended, turned up rear fuselage section also helps hide the exhaust from the ground. (Tony Landis)

The ball inside the housing just under the windscreen is the Forward Looking Infrared sensor turret. On the end of the nose are the four static pitot tubes which provide all air data to the flight control computer. (Author)

The wing trailing edge flaps (inboard) and elevons (outboard) work both independently and together. Even these movable control surfaces are faceted. (Tony Landis)

The twin all moving fins also act as twin rudders giving the F-117A good directional control. The 37th TFW markings, TR tail codes and the Tactical Air Command badge are all in Gray. (Tony Landis)

The large suck-in doors on top of the air intakes provide extra air to the engine during taxi and takeoff. This F-117A (842) was the 58th production aircraft and was delivered on 29 March 1990. The object just behind the fuselage insignia is a removable radar reflector. (Tony Landis)

The FLIR turret housing is covered with an NU metal screen that appears to radar as a solid flat panel. The rough areas around the framing are Radar Absorbent Material (RAM) putty used to cover fasteners around the FLIR frame. (Author)

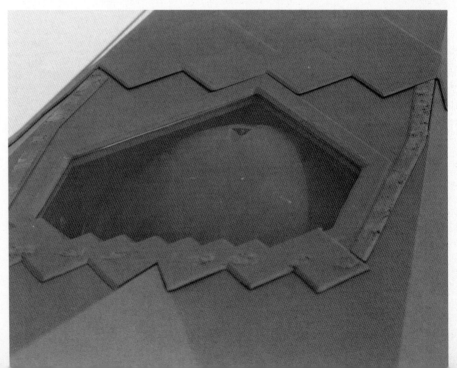

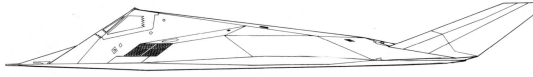

Specifications

Lockheed F-117A Stealth Fighter (Nighthawk)

Wingspan .43 feet 4 inches
Length . . . . .65 feet 11 inches
Height . . . . .12 feet 5 inches
Empty Weight . . . . .35,000 pounds
Maximum Weight . . . . .52,500 pounds
Powerplants. . . . . .Two 10,600 lbst General Electric
F404-F1D2 engines

Armament. . . . . .Two 2,000 pound bombs

Performance
  Maximum Speed . . . . .646 mph
  Service ceiling . . . . .45,000 Feet
  Range . . . . .1,000 miles
Crew . . . . .One

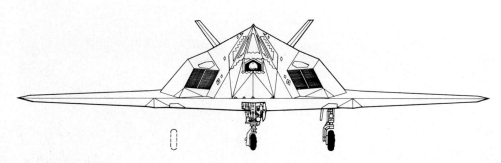

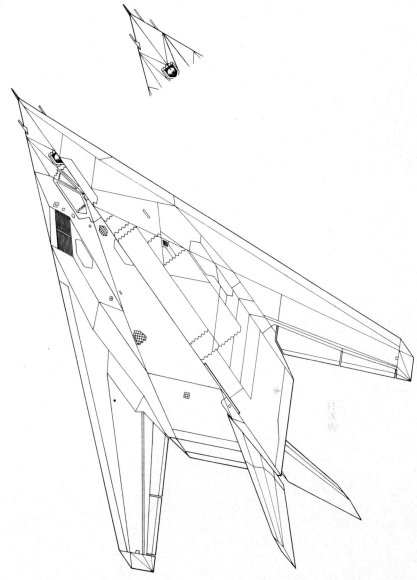

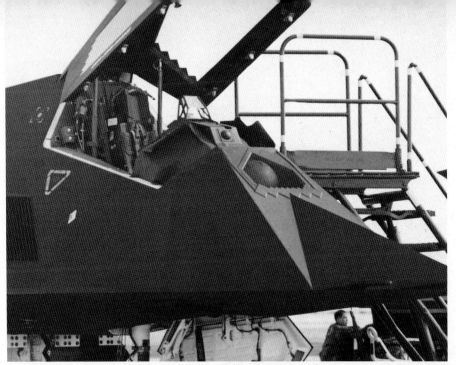

Each engine inlet is covered with two screen grids that are twenty-three openings wide and thirty-six openings high. The intake splitter plate is between the grids. The suck-in doors on the fuselage are spring loaded and open only when the engine needs additional air (taxi, ground runs and takeoff). (Tony Landis)

The Forward Looking Infrared (FLIR) is the primary target identification system on the F-117. The FLIR also provides a video image to the pilot during taxi and takeoff on blacked out airfields enabling him to find his way without the aid of external lights. (Author)

The F-117A cockpit is dominated by the large CRT displays used for the FLIR and DLIR. The FLIR/DLIR CRT is located between and below the standard five inch multi-function displays and is directly beneath the HUD key pad. The key pad just below the HUD is for calling up information onto the HUD display. (Tony Landis)

There is a retractable antenna immediately behind the main landing gear door. The landing gear and insides of all doors are White. The edges of all control surfaces are faceted, visbile on both the inboard and outboard evelons. (Tony Landis)

F-117A Into Service

The first operational F-117A pilots were selected during 1980 from candidates with more than 1,000 hours flight time, mostly in jet aircraft. Most were early to mid-career Captains that came from air-to-ground units flying F-4s, F-111s or A-10s. In mid-1982 the first pilots joined what is now the 37th Tactical Fighter Wing (originally known as the 4450th Tactical Group). One of the first tasks of these new pilots was to develop a training program for the F-117A. One of the most difficult aspects of flying the F-117A was that the pilot's first flight was at night (because of the secrecy surrounding the program). Day flights were almost completely prohibited, unless flown out of Groom Lake.

The F-117A was designed to operate primarily as a covert operations aircraft with organizations such as Delta Force. It would give these forces a first strike capability which could overfly hostile and/or friendly airspace without the permission or knowledge of the owner of that airspace. Its primary mission is precision attack against high value, highly defended targets. The aircraft was never designed to be used in large numbers, but rather a single aircraft against a single target at night — that is why it is painted overall Black.

The first operational group of F-117A pilots joined the 4450th in mid-1982. Initially, the unit started out with one squadron and as production increased, the unit was expanded from one squadron to two; originally known as Squadron A and Squadron B. The units had the nicknames "Nightstalkers" and "Grim Reapers." As more aircraft were delivered, the group went from two to three squadrons.

In October of 1989, the 37th Tactical Fighter Wing at George Air Force Base, California was deactivated and reactivated as the operational F-117A wing. The three squadrons were redesignated the 415th Tactical Fighter Squadron, the 416th Tactical Fighter Squadron and the 417th Tactical Fighter Training Squadron. Each squadron consists of approximately eighteen aircraft, with the exception of the training squadron which has the remaining flyable aircraft (usually six to ten aircraft). Typically, ten or eleven aircraft are in maintenance at one time.

Pilots commuted weekly from Las Vegas/Nellis Air Force Base to TTR (Monday through Friday). Monday was considered a light night with the other three flying nights being more active with each flyable aircraft flying two sorties per night. Training sorties are quite demanding. Although the aircraft was easy to fly, each training sortie lasted approximately ninety minutes and covered much of the western United States.

Since becoming operational, the 37th Tactical Fighter Wing has maintained a select group of aircraft as provisionally operational aircraft. They are identified by maintenance as being fully updated with all mandatory change orders and systems upgrades. These are the aircraft ready to go to war and there are generally five or six aircraft always listed as mission ready. In times of increased tension, other aircraft could be readied within 48 to 72 hours.

The 15 January 1991 issue of "Aviation Week," in their "Update Section," reported that the Air Force was asking Lockheed for a proposal aimed at reopening the F-117A production line to build at least one additional squadron (this was prior to the beginning of hostilities in Iraq). The aircraft has since proven itself in combat and it would not surprise the author if the F-117A was put back into procution; however, it would be a surprise if the number actually produced was released.

An F-117A (793) taxies out of its hangar at the Tonopah Test Range. There are fifty-four individual aircraft hangars in addition to maintenance hangars. This F-117A was the ninth production aircraft, delivered to the USAF on 1 February 1983. (Eric Schulzinger)

An F-117A (796) on final approach to Tonopah Test Range. For day flights the Stealth fighter normally keeps its retractable communications antennas deployed. (Eric Schulzinger)

A pair of F-117As taxi out on the taxiway at the Tonopah Test Range for night flying on the Nellis range. The small bulge on the fuselage side of the aircraft is a detachable radar reflector, installed so that local Air Traffic Control radars can track the F-117A. (Eric Schulzinger)

This F-117A (828), being prepared for an evening mission, is the personal aircraft of the commander of the 37th TFW and carries full unit markings on the fin in Light Gray. It was the forty-fourth production aircraft, delivered on 17 June 1987. (Eric Schulzinger)

14

These are some of the hangars for the F-117As of the 37th TFW at Tonopah. Each hangar houses a single F-117A and they normally are closed during the day. The area around Tonapah is typical of the Nevada desert — very empty. (Author)

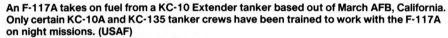

An F-117A takes on fuel from a KC-10 Extender tanker based out of March AFB, California. Only certain KC-10A and KC-135 tanker crews have been trained to work with the F-117A on night missions. (USAF)

While one ground crewman signals the pilot to stop on the taxiway at Tonopah, another prepares to put the wheel chocks in place around the nosewheel. This F-117A is aircraft Number 807. (Eric Schulzinger)

15

F-117A Losses

The first known F-117A loss took place on 20 April 1982 during the acceptance flight by LTC Bob Ridenhauer of the Number One production aircraft. The aircraft had performed adequately during predelivery testing; however, just prior to delivery Lockheed and the Air Force had instituted a number of major improvements and upgrades. One of these was the relocation of the stabilization augmentation system equipment from one equipment bay to another.

A primary consideration when building the F-117A was an attempt to engineer out the "What can go wrong, will go wrong," Murphy's Law syndrome. Lockheed designed the aircraft so that it could be put together in only one way and connectors can only go in one direction. But when they moved the flight data computer from one equipment bay to another, something went wrong.

When Bob Ridenhauer took off on the first acceptance flight, he found his controls were reversed. The pitch and yaw outputs were somehow reversed. The aircraft lost control, went inverted going backwards, and augered in on the side of the lake bed. Ridenhauer was stuck in the cockpit when the crash and rescue team arrived. They put the fire out and it took about twenty minutes to cut Bob from the aircraft. Bob Ridenhauer spent about eight months in the hospital at a cost to Lockheed and the Air Force of about $700,000. He is a very valuable, dedicated pilot, and lucky to be alive.

The airframe, Tail Number 785, now resides as a functional engineering airframe test fixture at the Lockheed Skunk Works in Burbank. At one time it was under consideration to be converted to a two seat trainer, but this program was cancelled.

The Second Loss

On the night of 11 June 1986 the Number Eight production F-117A, Tail Number 792, launched on a training mission at 0113 hours. The pilot, MAJ Ross E. Mulhare, had informed his colleagues that he was tired, and "Just couldn't shake it." He was the last aircraft on the evening's flight schedule. The mission route went south and west over the Sierra mountains, south of the San Joaquin Valley, and southeast towards the weapons range at Edwards Air Force Base.

As the pilots made their easterly turn, the lights of Bakersfield, California disappeared and were replaced by the darkness of the mountains around Tehachapi. At approximately 0145, Mulhare's F-117A entered into a steep dive (and could have been supersonic even though the F-117A is a subsonic aircraft) and hit the top of a mountain some seventeen miles northeast of Bakersfield.

MAJ Mulhare made no attempt to eject and was killed. Upon impact, the F-117A totally disintegrated. One of the unique features of the F-117A, unlike other USAF fighters, is that it has a flight data recorder. Even though Mulhare's F-117A was reduced to bits and pieces the size of a beer can, it was reported that the flight data recorder was recovered intact.

A recovery team was immediately summoned to the crash site and the area was cordoned off. They took the impact point, went out a thousand feet from the last bit of recognizable debris, then dug and sifted through every cubic foot of dirt in the area. After successfully retrieving every piece of the F-117A, the recovery crew (to put scavengers

and the media on a wrong course) took the remains of a crashed F-101A Voodoo that had been at Groom Lake for over twenty years and had it broken up. Then they went back to the site and scattered the debris of the old F-101 throughout the area. Anyone who later found pieces of an aircraft did not find pieces of the F-117A — they found pieces of the old McDonnell F-101A.

Loss Number Three

The last known crash of an F-117A was production number 31, Tail Number 815. It was lost on the night of 14 October 1987 on the Nellis Range just east of the Tonopah Test Range, approximately halfway between TTR and Groom Lake.

MAJ Michael C. Stewart left from the Tonopah Test Range Facility at 1953 hours and crashed into gently sloping ground on the Nellis Range some forty minutes later. Like MAJ Mulhare, Stewart made no attempt to eject and the aircraft was totally destroyed. The investigation focused once again on crew fatigue and disorientation. It was a clear night with no moon and there were no lights to help distinguish the ground. Reportedly, the mission included some special requirements which were deleted from the accident report. Once again, there were no substantial changes in operations after the accident. It's also believed that Stewart was possibly going supersonic when he crashed and that he had become disoriented.

Two F-117As (828 and 790) taxi in to the ramp at Nellis Air Force Base. The aircraft in the foreground has the brake chute container doors at the base of the fin open. The interior of the container well and the insides of the doors are in Gloss White. (Author)

F-117A Pilot Interviews

I was fortunate to have the opportunity to be the only person to (legally) interview, in depth, an F-117A pilot — Steve Paulson.

Steve was one of the original fifteen pilots chosen at the beginning of the program. He was responsible for flight tests, expanding the envelope and writing all the criteria for new pilot selection and training. He spent four years in the program and stated that it was the most exciting time he ever had.

Steve was brought to my attention through a friend in the Minnesota Air Guard, where I am the Wing Historian. I initially contacted Steve Paulson during mid-1989, told him who I was, what I wanted to do, and asked if he would be willing to be interviewed on tape. He said he would have to check with the security people at Tonopah and the local FBI office to get a clarification of what he could and could not say.

In mid-August 1989, we sat down with a list of 120 questions that I had put together. I would ask the questions and if he felt uncomfortable with the question or he did not want to answer it, he would say "no comment" or "next question." As it turned out, he answered most of the 120 questions along with a few additional questions. I asked if he would be willing to allow me to come back to discuss what a typical day for an F-117A pilot was like. He agreed, although he said he had to check with security, but he didn't see where there would be major problem. In November of 1989, I interviewed Steve a second time, learning what an F-117A pilot went through on a typical day.

As part of my responsibility as a member of the Air Guard, I submitted a transcript of my two interviews to Ben Rich, President of the Lockheed Skunk Works, to make sure that what I did would not jeopardize national security. Ben, in turn, sent it off to the Air Force Office of Special Investigation in Washington.

Overall, other articles and information written about the F-117A by myself have been well received. What we have in this Squadron/Signal publication is two never before published interviews with an F-117A pilot. The person who heads up the special projects group is COL Barry Henessey, while the civilian director of security for all *Senior* programs is Pete Eames. Pete reviewed it, did not like what was there, but opted not to respond.

On 3 September 1990, I was called to active duty for Operation DESERT SHIELD, spending two and one half months at the National Guard Bureau in Washington D.C. When I arrived at the Pentagon, I needed to get my security clearance validated to get a permanent Pentagon pass.

There was a problem with my clearance and they wouldn't tell me why. I finally contacted Pete Eames and spent about two hours with him discussing my love of aircraft — and why he doesn't like me. He felt that my questions were too good and he didn't like that at all. I informed him that, "This is America. It is my right to ask questions. Your concern should be the answers I get to those questions." We did leave on fairly good terms and the interviews were cleared (although the Air Force has put restrictions on any future interviews).

F-117A Pilot Interview Number One

Jim: When did you enter the Program?

Steve: I interviewed for it in 1980 and got out to Vegas in June of 1982. During the interview, they wouldn't tell us what the program was. They gave us some hints what we would be doing; we would be gone all week, in a secret program, flying A-7s. Then they gave me about 5 minutes to decide. I didn't know I would have to wait two years for an answer and neither did they. They were starting to bring guys out there right then, but the aircraft got delayed. That delayed the whole program for a while and they didn't need anyone for a couple of years. None of the pilots arrived out there until just shortly before we got the production aircraft.

Photographer Tony Landis (left) and the author (right) in front of the main gate sign at the Tonopah Test Range. The base main gate is another eighteen miles down the road. The sign consists of the first stage booster from a Nike Ajax missile with a B-43 nuclear shape (bomb) on top. (Author)

Jim: Do you know how or why you were chosen?

Steve: *No, the first squadron commander, Robert J. Jackson, was picked to conduct the interviews. They wanted F-4, F-111 and A-10 guys, mostly with air-to-ground time. They wanted guys that were all in about the same age group, middle to senior Captains. Then, they looked through the records for the best pilots they could find and interviewed them.*

Jim: What was involved in the initial training for the F-117A?

Steve: *Lockheed was trying to do the academic and we used to go out to Burbank. Those guys taught maintenance courses; they didn't teach pilots courses. They taught wiring diagrams and things we didn't care about, nothing about flying. We all sat through all of that stuff a couple of times before we got into the aircraft. Then, once we got into the aircraft and starting flying, we built our own academic program.*

Jim: Did the *Have Blue* program teach you anything?

Steve: *No, the aircraft were different. They were smaller and were not the same exact shape either. The tails were different and there were other minor differences. The flying characteristics were not exactly the same either.*

Jim: Did you have a lot of simulator time before your first flight?

Steve: *We didn't have one yet. We had a CPT, just a cockpit layout but we didn't have a simulator.*

Jim: So, you didn't know how it would handle.

Steve: *No, not really. Our first guy, Al Whitley, flew it shortly after the test pilots flew it, after the*

This F-117A (789) has all its retractable communications antennas deployed. The Flat Black finish and RAM fade at different rates giving the aircraft a patchy appearance. Number 789 was the fifth production aircraft delivered on 17 November 1982. (Eric Schulzinger)

first flight of the second aircraft. Then we started flying it. Before we flew it the first time, we would go take a ride in an F-15 because the F-117A lands and takes off like an F-15. We would take one ride in the Eagle, then come back and fly the F-117A.

Jim: What was your impression of your first lift off?

Steve: *Smooth. It is the smoothest flying aircraft I have ever been in. It is smoother than the F-15 and that is strictly due to all the work they did with the flight control computers. The aircraft is fully fly-by-wire, like the F-16, but with a conventional center stick.*

Jim: I understand that the throttle quadrant is straight out of an A-10.

Steve: *I don't know, nobody ever mentioned it, but they used a lot of off-the-shelf things. I never heard any of the A-10 guys say that it was the same as an A-10, but they were big throttles.*

Jim: Did it have a big CRT with a couple of small ones on the side?

Steve: *Yes.*

Jim: Other than the CRTs, could the F-16 cockpit layout be considered as similar to the F-117A?

Steve: *No, not really because of the big thing in there, the sensor display, is right in the middle. It took priority over everything else, then you have the CRTs on both sides. You could punch up anything you wanted on both of those, any of your instruments and that is what you do your flying from.*

The special crew ladder is attached to the cockpit while a ground crewman walks back along the fuselage with protective covers on his shoes. Reportedly the boarding ladder was a commercial articulating folding ladder that actually saved the government money. (Author)

Jim: Do you know why the A-7 was chosen as the chase-plane?

Steve: *Originally they wanted the F-16, but it was too expensive. I forgot the real reason they settled on the A-7. I think one of the reasons was because it was easy to get at the time and that might have been the biggest reason. It also has a computer in it, but that is about where the similarity ends.*

Jim: In your opinion, shouldn't the designation have been A-something versus an F-something since it is an air to mud aircraft?

Steve: *Well, it has air-to-air capabilities. When I left, we hadn't trained with any of that, but they are still building and testing weapons for it all the time. Everything is carried internal.*

Jim: The F-117 was designed to complement the A-6 and A-7?

Steve: *Yes, I suppose. It is really a precision night attack bomber designed to take out high value targets.*

Jim: During the time frame that you were in the program, was the F-117 ever considered for an operational mission. I know they considered it for Libya, but Weinberger said it was too expensive to use.

Steve: *Yes, let's just say that we were within hours of going on two different occasions.*

Jim: In your opinion, was the program worth the cost, in terms of technology vs cost?

Steve: *Yes, it is cheap compared to the B-2. The Air Force originally wanted eighteen for a special squadron to do Delta Force type special projects where one or two aircraft would take out some high valued target without anybody knowing it. Congress decided it wanted a wing; they were the ones who made the Air Force buy fifty-nine aircraft. The Air Force never wanted that many. None of us even thought there was a use for two squadrons. It is really no good in a general war scenario and that was too many aircraft to use in a limited clandestine operation. They probably bought more than they needed, but there has been a great advance in technology. (DESERT STORM proved that theory wrong).*

Jim: Fifty-nine aircraft are listed in various sources; does that include the five pre-production aircraft?

Steve: *Well, it must. I think we got fifty-five production aircraft, so a fifty-nine total would probably include the preproduction aircraft.*

Jim: What does the FLIR/DLIR CRT give you as far as information?

Steve: *One is forward looking, mounted in front the of windscreen. The other is under the aircraft and is downward looking. Both are infrared and give you a visual display. It is mainly a sensor display used for bombing, not flying the aircraft.*

Jim: Do you wear night vision goggles if it is at night?

Steve: *No, we don't need them. We are not down at ten feet doing low level stuff at night. We looked into night vision goggles and found we really don't need them. They are not useful unless it is real dark. There is some input from the IR into the HUD so you can see where you are going.*

Jim: In other words, you would fly the F-117A at night the same way you would fly an F-15 or F-16?

Steve: *Yes, but it is quite a bit easier to fly at night than an F-15 or F-16 because of the systems on it, but you fly it somewhat the same.*

Jim Does it have a Honeywell ring laser gyro for navigation?

Steve: *No, it has a good INS. It uses a special (don't know who makes it, but I know what it is made out of) metal. It takes a long time to align, but due to that, it is very accurate.*

Jim: What type of conventional weapons does it carry?

Steve: *The primary weapon would be a laser-guided type bomb. Normally, two bombs at 2,000 pounds each.*

Jim: Someone in an issue of Air Force magazine said something about the BLU 109 penetrator weapon. Can that be carried?

Steve: *Again, we had some special weapons they were making specifically for the airplane, plus they had modified a lot of existing weapons. You have a certain internal space and if it fits in there, we can use it.*

Jim: When you drop the weapons, are you at a relatively high altitude?

Steve: *You don't have to be.*

Jim: Do the weapons bay doors open real fast, like an F-106 and are the bombs pneumatically ejected?

Steve: *No. The bombs just drop out.*

The port side weapons bay of an F-117A, with the weapons pylon lowered to the fully extended position. This pylon can carry up to 5,000 pounds of ordnance or fuel tanks. (Author)

Jim: When you are training, how much of your time was spent on tactics?

Steve: You mean actual flying time?

Jim: Yes.

Steve: We talked tactics everyday. Your initial training was doing a few benign things, i.e. learning how to fly the airplane and use the systems, but after that, it was all real training using tactics every night.

Jim: You said earlier that the aircraft was one of the best handling aircraft you have ever flown. In Aviation Week (Ben Rich calls it Aviation Leak), however, they call it the "Wobbly Goblin." Is there a reason for the name?

Steve: The only thing they may be alluding to is that if it departs, it departs in a real weird mode and they may call it the "Wobbly Goblin."

Jim: In other words, at a too high angle of attack...

Steve: It will depart. It hasn't happened that we know of, but they did tests on it with a model. The aircraft is real responsive. It doesn't roll as fast as an F-15 or have the thrust of an F-15, but the actual stick feel is smoother than an F-15. It has certain restrictions on it as far as air speed, both upper and lower ends, and angle of attack because it is unstable. If you do get a speed stall or departed, it won't recover. It is not like an F-15 where you can recover. Once it departs, it is gone.

Jim: What would be involved in a deployment? I was told that the wings can be removed for delivery to forward operating locations.

Steve: Unless it was a real long lead time evolution, we would probably fly out. But when they brought the aircraft out to us initially, it was in C-5s with the wings removed.

Ground crewmen remove Red protective covers on the wing leading edge just after removing the boarding ladder. These covers insure that the ladder does not damage the leading edge RAM. (Author)

Jim: If you were to deploy overseas would it be typically one aircraft or two. Was there a typical scenario worked out? (This question was answered on 19 August 1990 when the first of forty-two F-117As left for Saudia Arabia).

Steve: No, not typical. It would depend on the situation. They had a lot of plans and were drawing up a lot of plans on how to use the F-117A and how to integrate it with regular forces for a large scale war time scenario. Although it is going to be years before they practice that stuff, like a Red Flag or anything. But it depends on the scenario. Normally, because of its mission, you would go with just a couple of aircraft.

Jim: There are the static pitot tubes on the nose which I assume are a quadredundant air data system, but I am not sure.

Steve: That is pretty close. You cannot tell from pictures exactly but there is no angle of attack probes or any other stuff that would create a radar return. Those four probes supply all the information to fly the airplane.

Jim: I understand that they are plastic, square in shape with a metallic coating.

Steve: They are something like that. Initially, they couldn't figure out how to heat them and not disrupt the air flow going through there and get weird readings. When we first started to fly the airplane, they were not heated. That meant you couldn't go near a cloud until they figured out how to heat them, which they have done.

Jim: What would an attack profile be on a simulated target? Would you come in high and stay high?

Steve: It is all dependent on the defenses. Certain radars you would want to be low on, certain radars it is best to go in high and right at them or some at medium altitude and right at them. We knew what all those were and we had billions of dollars in computer systems there for us to figure out our route for any place we wanted to go. The computer would pick out the best route in and out to avoid radars or to tell you what altitude to be at, to be the least susceptible to them.

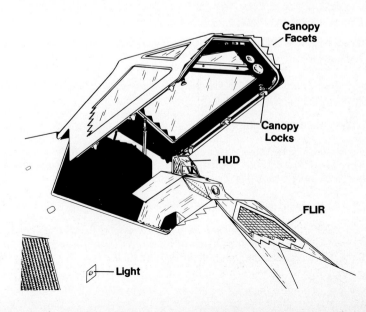

Canopy Facets

Canopy Locks

HUD

FLIR

Light

Jim: Your weapons delivery would be from straight and level, or a dive. Did it make any difference?

Steve: *Normally, it would be from straight and level. It would be the easiest way to do it.*

Jim: Were the preproduction aircraft called the F-117s and the production variants called F-117As?

Steve: *Not really. Everything says F-117A on it.*

Jim: How many aircraft are launched during a typical cycle?

Steve: *First off, we only had one airplane. By the time I left, we had about thirty-eight of them. We had a whole squadron and were just starting a second squadron, so we would fly maybe eighteen sorties with eight primary aircraft and two spares.*

Jim: What is the normal complement of pilots at TTR?

Steve: *Again, that has grown. We had a squadron of eighteen primary aircraft with six backups, twenty-four total. We were always undermanned because we were growing. I imagine that there is a pilot to aircraft ratio of 1.25 like the air force wants, which would be 25-30 pilots in each squadron.*

Jim: What is the normal tour of duty with the unit?

Steve: *It is three years now. It was four.*

Jim: Do they take them from the normal ranks as a rotational thing, provided they have the background and flying time?

Steve: *I am not sure what they are doing right now. They still hand pick most of the pilots. What we did was to recommend a guy or they would bring in fifteen names to see if we knew them and would recommend one for interview.*

Jim: Was it a good group of guys overall?

Steve: *Yeah, it was real good. Now they have two squadrons, it is a lot bigger and they are having more problems just because they have a lot more people. Again, the original was fifteen hand picked guys all ready to go. We had it easier in the beginning - it was kind of a flying club. We didn't have any rules, no regulations until we started crashing aircraft. Then they started putting some rules into effect.*

Jim: Was it fatiguing to fly at night?

Steve: *The actual flying wasn't, but the hours that we flew were. You know that when you get out and climb into the aircraft, your adrenaline is so high that you don't get tired while you are flying, but then you land and it is 3 AM and you get real tired.*

Jim: Because it is a stealth aircraft, obviously everything is internal. Was there ever any consideration of having anything external?

Steve: *No, for long range ferry flights, we put fuel tanks internal instead of weapons.*

Jim: Is the platypus moveable?

Steve: *It is not movable, although it does expand quite a bit.*

Jim: Is the bottom surface, for all intents and purposes, flat?

Steve: *There are some facets in certain areas that are not perfectly flat. In fact, the whole thing angles in like a boat bottom, it is deeper in the middle and you can see a little V angle in a few places.*

Jim: I understand the only round portion of the aircraft is the very top of the canopy where they put the crash recorder.

Steve: *That is about right. It is just where everything comes together and there is a slight curve to it.*

Ground crews tow an F-117A (842) to a secure hangar for the night. F-117As are rarely, if ever, parked out in the open for any period of time. Most of the time, they are safely hidden inside secure hangars, away from prying eyes. (Tony Landis)

Jim: You don't seem to have much head room.

Steve: *It gets narrow up there; you can move your head five inches from side to side without hitting the side.*

Jim: I overlooked the facility, due north of the tower, and could see the rows of hangars. I am assuming that there is a hangar for each aircraft. Is that correct?

Steve: *Yes.*

Jim: One evening when I was there, there was a lot of activity. When they flew at night, did they normally take off at sunset?

Steve: *No, we couldn't open the hangar doors until half an hour after twilight, which was a few minutes either side of sunset. I can't remember which side it was now. But you couldn't open the doors until half an hour after that so it was pretty dark. You couldn't start the engines until after the doors were open, so we never took off until at least an hour after sunset. They would open the door thirty minutes after a light sensor said there was no direct sunlight hitting the source.*

Jim: Was your first flight at night?

Steve: *No, we did our training at Groom.*

Jim: Was there a reason they built Tonapah Test Range rather than keeping the operations at Groom?

Steve: *Yes, they were never planning to keep operations at Groom. That was just too much going on there. I assume that they are all out of there, now that they can fly during the day at Tonapah. That is a systems command base, basically.*

Jim: I understand that the F-117A's top speed is limited to Mach .82 to .84. Can it go faster than that?

Steve: *Yes, there is an artificial limit that we set that is a little higher than that just so we wouldn't go too fast.*

Jim: Is it capable of supersonic flight?

Steve: *It is capable.*

Jim: Are you limited because of delamination of the RAM?

Steve: *No, there is a limit there and a reason for it, but it has to do with the way you get inputs to your flight control system.*

Jim: What are the G limits on the aircraft?

Steve: *Comparable to the F-4 and T-38.*

Jim: Is the HUD typical to what is available on other fighters or is it unique?

Steve: *It is typical. Again, it presents different information than what you would get in, say an F-*

An F-117A (842) of the 37th TFW is pulled out of the transit hangar at Andrews Air Force Base, Washington D.C. on 19 May 1990. The tow bar is attached to the nosewheel. This was the next to last F-117A delivered to the Air Force. (Tony Landis)

15, but it is a better HUD than the stock -15. It is not as good as the F-15E, but it is a pretty good HUD and has all the information you will every want on there, plus 50% more than we ever want.

Jim: I am assuming that the F-117A has multiple backups as far as flight computers, etc. Were they fairly reliable during the time frame that you flew?

Steve: *Yes, we rarely had flight control problems. We never had anything major, everything was minor. I had one of the first and biggest emergencies that we had and it wasn't that big of a deal. After takeoff one night, I put the gear up and the lights stayed on. They didn't come up. And my hydraulic pressure went to zero. There was a Y fitting where two systems come together. It had broken right at the Y and pumped out all the hydraulic fluid. Well, none of us had ever seen this before, so I went into a holding pattern and started talking about the warning lights I had. We thought all the lights weren't lighting up, but it was that certain ones light up and then go out to tell you which systems you lost, just the way the book said they were supposed to. We talked about that for a while. Basically, I just burned down gas, came in and landed.*

Jim: Did the gear ever retract?

Steve: *No, they had come part way up, then stopped, so I used an emergency extension, just blowing them down like any other aircraft. Pulling the handle and basically a free fall down. I came in and landed, then used the emergency brake, reserve brake pressure, to stop. It wasn't that big a deal, but we found out that some of the things they put in the book didn't match up with what actually happened in the aircraft when we saw it for real. It was kind of a learning process the whole time with a new aircraft.*

Jim: What is the combat radius?

Steve: *Well, let me think - actually I have really forgotten. If you figure 12,000 pounds of gas, it burns about the same as anything else at altitude, i.e. about 3,000 pounds an hour or so. An hour out and an hour back is about your maximum, that is 400-500 miles. But with air refueling, you could go as far as you want.*

Jim: Are the refueling doors on the fuselage top a rotating type door and is refueling relatively easy?

Steve: *That is correct. The refueling is not easy because of the canopy, it is like flying low and going in turns. Your visibility quits right here and there is no canopy up here. It is all metal, so you can't see above you. Your front visibility is restricted so you can't see the tanker very well. You can't see anything out the top and you can't see the boom like we do in a normal fighter. Refueling wasn't hard, but some guys had problems with it. Another thing, it is all at night.*

Jim: Does the F-117A use standard JP4?

Steve: *Yes.*

Jim: Do you recall what aircraft had the American flag on the bottom?

Steve: *I remember it. I think it was probably 782, one of the first aircraft. I remember seeing it.*

Jim: Did the painting cover the whole bottom?

Steve: *Yes, pretty much of it. It believe it was when Weinberger was there and they painted it for his fly-by.*

Jim: Is the F-117A called the Nighthawk?

Steve: *Yes.*

Jim: Is this an official name, like the Eagle or Hornet?

Steve: *I don't know.*

Jim: Was there ever a designation of F-19?

Steve: *The story we got is that the F-117A designation was a mistake. The 117 was a generic term they use up North for all new aircraft and test pilot flying that they don't have a name for, like the guys flying the MiGs out there used to be 117 time, because they couldn't designate anything else. So, when they first started building the aircraft, they called it the 117 until they could give it a real name. Well, Lockheed printed up the first Dash One Pilot Maual with F-117A on it. So, the Air Force said they wouldn't pay millions of dollars to re-do it, so it became the F-117A. That is how it got its designation. It probably would have been the F-19. It was all a mistake.*

Jim: When you were at Groom, were there other Stealth aircraft flying from other manufacturers?

Steve: *No, there were other aircraft there being tested that were stealthy, but for different jobs. There was no competition between those aircraft and the F-117A. It was for a totally different purpose.*

Jim: I understand that on one F-117A flight the aircraft lost one of the rudders. How did the aircraft handle?

Steve: *Excellent.*

This F-117A is in position for refueling, the fuel overflow vents are visible on either side of the refueling port. There is a retractable antenna to the left of the refueling port and a rotating beacon to the right. The trailing edge of the platypus exhaust tiles have been filled in with a high temperature sealant. (Mike Dornheim)

Jim: Then the flight control system compensated for it?

Steve: Yes, there was no difference whatsoever.

Jim: Did it physically come off?

Steve: It broke off at high speed. It was during a test flight, they were doing some other stuff. It went pop and broke off — the whole thing. It is all on file, they were filming the whole thing.

Jim: At Groom, did they film most of the takeoffs and landings?

Steve: Yeah, they always have all the cameras running. When there were more aircraft than cameras, that's what they don't get. Otherwise, they are always filming.

Jim: I understand that one of the F-117As got hit by lightning on the nose and it had one static pitot tube left when the guy brought it in - or only one operating.

Steve: Yes, it was hit and it did some damage. I don't remember how many tubes he had left, although it didn't affect the flying of the aircraft at all.

Jim: Because the cockpit is the largest infrared signature in the aircraft other than the exhausts, is there something they did with the windscreen or the canopy?

Steve: That is why it is shaped the way it is. It doesn't have rounded edges at all, it is a window. Your head is a fairly big radar reflector in there, but that is one of the reasons that it is not open on top. And why they don't have a regular canopy there, because then radar would pick up the guy instead of the aircraft.

Jim: Do they always use drag chutes for the landings? Do you use aerodynamic braking?

Steve: No, once it is on the ground, it is on the ground and you cannot aero brake it. That had to do with the flight controls. As a normal occurrence, we used a drag chute all the time, unless there was too much crosswind. It can land without one, but it's hard on the brakes. The brakes are extremely good; however, they are changing the wheel assemblies. The brakes were made of a carbon material that would get, under moderate braking, red hot. When you would pull off the runway and sit there for a few minutes, the brakes would burst into flames. So, anytime you landed without a chute and without a head wind, you would have to sit in a hot brake area for a minute to make sure your brakes where not going to flame up. It was good material, it was just real susceptible to fire.

Jim: If you went to Europe, that would be an awfully long haul in the aircraft. Would you dismantle it and ship it over in a C-5?

Steve: No, we would fly it with a tanker. It is a lot easier than taking it apart. We have flown long missions, around twelve hours. There weren't any problems with the reliability. We had minor problems with the electronics once in a while - the computers went crazy. There were hydraulic problems once in a while, but all in all, there were the typical problems with the FLIR and the DLIR and the weapons system — trying to integrate all the stuff to make it exact, real accurate. But the basic air frame flew very well.

Jim: On a high angle attack do you have problems not getting enough air in the inlets since it is sloped back?

Steve: No, those suck-in doors open up anytime you need them, but it is mainly just for takeoff.

Jim: In a combat situation, if you had an air-to-air weapon, would it be an effective aircraft? Is it maneuverable?

Steve: Yes, it is real maneuverable. There is a low wing load - it is just like the B-2, it is all wing. A real low wing load. The problem is engine thrust, you lose a lot of it with all the fancy crap on there.

An F-117A (828) lands at Nellis Air Force Base, Nevada, during its first public press conference. The drag chute is normally used on F-117A landings and is Black. The bright spots on the landing gear legs are the approach and landing lights. (Author)

Eye witnesses reported that this F-117 was painted with an American flag covering the entire undersurfaces and the Lockheed Skunk Works logo on the fin when the aircraft was officially unveiled to high ranking officials, including the Secretary of Defense, Casper Weinberger.

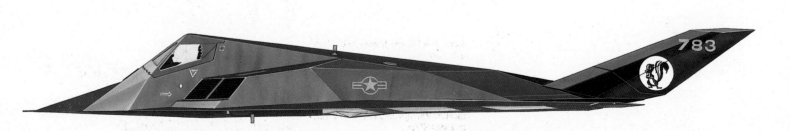

37th TACTICAL FIGHTER WING

415th TACTICAL FIGHTER SQUADRON

416th TACTICAL FIGHTER SQUADRON

417th TACTICAL FIGHTER TRAINING SQUADRON

Lockheed Company Patches worn by program support personnel.

4450th TACTICAL GROUP

Squadron A "NIGHT STALKERS"

Squadron B "GRIM REAPERS"

The "GOAT SUCKERS" patch was an early 4450th TG patch worn by F-117 pilots when engaged with the unit's A-7s.

Unit markings for F-117As are carried on the fin in Light Gray.

These patches were designed for F-117A crews assigned to Operation DESERT SHIELD/DESERT STORM.

COL AL WHITLEY

Aircraft 813 was flown by COL Al Whitley and carried the name *THE TOXIC AVENGER* on the inside of the weapons bay door. When the unit returned to Nellis AFB, it carried twenty-nine mission markings under the cockpit in Light Gray.

THE TOXIC AVENGER

Preproduction F-117s carried special markings on their fins during their test period. Aircraft 782 carried a White Playboy Bunny on the fin.

F-117A (790) rolls out at Nellis AFB, Nevada, on 21 April 1990 with its drag chute fully deployed. The bright spot on the upper fuselage is the removable Red rotating beacon, not used on normal missions. (Author)

Jim: Did you have a number of retractable antennas on the aircraft?

Steve: Yes, all the antennas were retractable - UHF, everything.

Jim: The RAM was laid on much like linoleum, but I understand that later on they had it fixed so it was sprayed on.

Steve: They hadn't started doing that when I left, but they were going to do the whole aircraft like that. They could spray on small areas, they just couldn't do the whole plane yet. The other problem was that the RAM's backing was different kinds of metal for different areas on the aircraft. There was pretty thick stuff, but it wasn't just plastic, there was a metal backing on a lot of it.

Jim: Not counting the RAM, was the external skin a composite?

Steve: Most of it was aluminum.

Jim: Had they flown any aircraft without any RAM at all?

Steve: I never saw any without any RAM. I don't think so.

Jim: Have you ever flown with AWACs?

Steve: Using AWACs or against them?

Jim: Simulated against them?

Steve: Yes, we did it.

Jim: Did they even know you were there?

Steve: Just about any radar can pick us up somewhere, it just depends on what range. There is a area that they can see us.

Jim: I assume that because they have a relatively small antenna, that you would be virtually invisible to most Soviet look down/shoot down type radars.

Steve: Yes, you could probably say that. It is pretty good. Again, the different edges, like the leading edges, have a different kind of RAM on them than different trailing edges in different parts of the aircraft. It has to be a compromise against all radars, so some of the super radars like Tall Kings with real long wave lengths can see at different ranges. It might be better against you at different altitudes than something like an F-15 radar with a real high PRF and short frequency.

Jim: Is there no radar in this aircraft at all?

Steve: No, there has been a lot of discussion on that. I don't know if they are still planning on doing that.

Jim: Where would you put it?

Steve: We were going to put it up in the nose. They did a lot of testing on synthetic aperture radar.

Jim: At what speed do you take off, when you rotate?

Steve: Fairly fast, because there is not much in the way of lifting devices.

Jim: Around 180 knots?

Steve: Close to that.

Jim: Is the landing speed about the same?

Steve: Landing is a lot slower just because you have less weight, but it is still above 150.

Jim: Everything built in recent years has an arresting hook. Does the aircraft have a hook?

Steve: Yes, it is internal and small, like an F-15.

Jim: Did any of you guys ever have to use the arresting hook?

Steve: Practiced. They did a couple of tests with it. We never used it. I could probably have taken it the night I had the hydraulic failure just because that is what the procedure calls for, but we didn't need it. We never had to take it because of an emergency in the air. It was tested, yes.

Jim: Did they have any other people from other branches of the service flying the aircraft?

Steve: Yes, we had a SAC guy.

F-117A Pilot Interview Number Two

Jim: What was Tonapah like as a place to be based? Was it non-family duty?

Steve: No, it was a family base. In the beginning, of course, they were still building it. It had just a small chow hall and we lived out in winterized trailers more or less.

Jim: Was it on the main part of the base?

Steve: It was on the main part of the base. That was built right away. The housing area was seven miles away from the base. That was done to keep the cooks and cleaners away from the main part of the base.

Jim: Is that what I see when I go up to the main gate out at Tonapah?

Steve: You see the housing area.

Jim: In off duty time, did you generally stay there or did you head back to Las Vegas? What was the normal routine?

Steve: Normally, a typical week would vary by a few hours, depending on whether it was winter or summer. Because we did all of our flying at night, we would leave Monday afternoon, head out to Tonapah from Nellis and come home Friday morning or afternoon. We were gone all week. If you had to get back you could, because they had shuttles running up until about 1700 every night.

Jim: I have seen the Key Airlines' shuttle going in there constantly.

Steve: That's what we would go back and forth on, but we flew at night so we would be done late in the morning. The Key flights don't come in until 0800 or 0900 in the morning so you couldn't go home and fly that night again, so we stayed there all week.

A Key Airlines 727 takes off from Nellis Air Force Base for the flight to Tonapah. The airline ran a government contract shuttle operation for aircrews living at Nellis/Las Vegas. (Author)

This sign welcomed visitors to the town of Tonopah, Nevada. Of course, there was no mention of the Tonopah Test Facility and the 37th TFW. (Author)

Jim: What did you do during your leisure time?

Steve: *I would normally get up about 1000 and Wayne Mudge and I would go out and play tennis, unless it was snowing, then we'd go eat lunch. Then we normally had a couple of hours, again depending whether it was winter or summer, just to screw around.*

Jim: Did you ever go into the town of Tonapah?

Steve: *Again, early on we could go in there. Nobody did too much, I was downtown twice I guess. Some of the maintenance guys could get in there more often. It was kind of discouraged, they didn't want a lot of Air Force guys running around town. It was not that we were absolutely forbidden, it was just that it was hard to do and it was discouraged.*

Jim: What were the other pilots like? Strong individuals? You guys all had a common background?

Steve: *They were all picked for flying ability among other things I guess, and decision making. They had to be able to get through any unknown emergencies because it was a brand new aircraft and they didn't know a lot about it when they first started flying it. So, they had to be calm people and decent pilots. They basically came from three pilot groups F-4s, F-111s and A-10s.*

Jim: Are there differences among pilot types between air-to-ground or air-to-air?

Steve: *Not really, not pilot types. It is just what you are used to doing. In the F-4, you flew both air-to-ground and air-to-air. In the F-111 and the A-10 you didn't, it was strictly air-to-ground. It is not a difference in pilot types, just what you were exposed to.*

Jim: While you were at Tonapah, how many different commanders did you have?

Steve: *There was only one at a time, but over my four years there, there were a number of different ones.*

Jim: Were they pretty good?

Steve: *Yes, the squadron commanders were real good. The wing commanders and group commanders were picked, I would say, politically -somebody's favorite boy on his way up to being General. I would say they had limited flying background because they were fast burners, had a lot of staff jobs. They were one step below a general so they didn't have a good flying background and probably didn't do a lot for operations, i.e. flying ops. But they did good for a brand new unit where they had to put everything together, not just the flying operations. They had to put the whole base together. They were good that way, they were not especially good for us - the flyers.*

Jim: Was there a common factor other than the one you already mentioned?

Steve: *No, that was about it. They were fast burners. Because of that they seemed to have a whole lot of family problems. Two of them got divorced, I think, while they were there or afterwards. It didn't have anything to do with the job so much but rather their personalities and the kind of guy they got for the job.*

Jim: How did security affect your day to day operations?

Steve: *It was extremely important. The building we operated out of didn't have any windows. It*

A ground crewman directs an F-117A into its parking spot on the ramp at Nellis Air Force Base during the aircraft's first public display. The small bulges on the fuselage sides are detachable radar reflectors. (Author)

was one big vault, plus the area where we kept all of our flight manuals was a separate room which was a vault - so a vault within a vault with combination locks, etc. You could get in there, take your flight manuals out of there, study them but you couldn't leave them anywhere, even in the building. If you didn't physically have them in your hand, you had to give them to someone while you went to the bathroom, etc. or put them back in the vault.

Jim: Even if everyone in the vault was cleared?

Steve: *Everyone in the building wasn't cleared. There were secretaries there. They were cleared to work there, but they didn't have "the need to know."*

Jim: During the time frame that you were there, were there ever any instances where someone, an outsider, tried to penetrate the defense line or got onto the base?

Steve: *I remember the cops chasing a couple of guys who had gotten onto the base. They would call a trooper alert once in a while, but it was real rare. Nobody ever got to the main base, or to the flying part of the base that I know of. At night, if they would see a truck up in the hills or somebody who came too close, they would go find out who it was. I don't recall any intruders getting onto the base. Now they had - and I recall only one specific instance because I chased them in the Mitsubishi for a while - one guy in a light aircraft. They tracked anything that went near Tonapah or in the box. He was suspicious around the borders or maybe even went through Tonapah air space. I was in the Mitsubishi heading up to Tonapah at the time and got a call from Dreamland to get his tail numbers etc., which we did. They tracked him and had FBI meet him when he landed, I think in Phoenix, although I don't remember where he landed. He turned out be a German or Bulgarian with tons of camera equipment. He had a story that he was on some sightseeing tour and got lost, but he was trying to get pictures of the facility. They kept real close track.*

Jim: Now today if someone wanted to fly in non-restricted air space but right along the very edge.

Steve: *You can do that. There are airways that go along the north edge and the west edge. It is legal to do, but if anybody is in those airways, normally they are talking to center. Or, if they are VFR and as long as they stay outside the area restrictions, they are fine. But if they come in the Nellis air space at all, that is when they become suspicious and start getting looked at.*

29

An F-117A (790) taxies in at Nellis Air Force Base past A-10 Thunderbolt IIs and an F-15E Strike Eagle. Most F-117A pilots came from the air-to-ground community and formerly flew A-10s, F-4s or A-7s. (Author)

Jim: I have been told that the F-117A is not an Air Force asset and the service doesn't order its use. In this case, who does?

Steve: It is an Air Force asset. The biggest problem is defining a real mission for it which did take a few years. What they were originally going to use it for, because the Air Force didn't want that many as I told you before, was different from what it ended up being because they had so many of them. I don't know if they ever did define a realistic mission for fifty-nine of them. They are not going to be of real use in a general war, but they are an Air Force asset. One of the big problems was letting other theater commanders, like guys in Europe and PACAF know that it is available without giving away too much, it was still highly secret then. In one sense, you had a real high-value asset that nobody knew about or how to implement and put it in with their own forces if they needed to use it.

Jim: In the time frame that you were there, did any F-117As ever physically operate outside the continental United States? Or do you think they have since?

Steve: No, I don't think so. We had a couple bases around the world we could go to, but the only reason to bring it out of the U.S. is if you are going to use it. They would do that at the last minute. You can use it from the U.S. for a lot of missions.

Jim: Most missions were at night until this year. Did you as a pilot adapt to the nocturnal life style?

Steve: You did, but you never did it well. Like I said, we would go to work from the main camp in the winter around 1 pm. In the summer, you might go in at 1600 or 1700 because you couldn't start flying until dark. In the winter, your first takeoff might be 1900; in the summer, it might not be until 2130.

Jim: Was the whole base set up around that?

Steve: It should have been but it wasn't. There was support for flying ops at night, but as the base grew bigger and bigger, there were all the functions that you have on a normal base. One of the big problems was that the main activities of the base operated on a daytime schedule, whereas all the pilots and operations were on a nighttime schedule. That created some problems.

Jim: How long did it take to prepare for a simulated mission? Can I assume that during the time you were there, that there was nothing actual and that everything was simulated?

Steve: Yes, for simulated missions we would have a mass briefing at night. This was when I was there, although we changed it a few times and may have since changed it. For the most part, you would have a mass briefing at night that showed the routes you were going to fly that night and there might be a couple of different ones, or everybody might be flying one route. It depended on what night and what we were doing and the weather, etc. Somebody would brief the routes, the targets on the route, the weather and the other general things that went along with a briefing that normally would have been done one on one. Then, the pilots left to go do target study and route study and different things like that, and get themselves ready for their mission. It was just a single ship mission, so you didn't have anyone else to brief. We did it like a normal briefing, around 2 hours prior to takeoff.

Jim: During your preparation for a simulated mission at any time did you use flight simulators?

Steve: No, they do have one though. Just before I left, they got it completed so they do have one there now. Prior to that, we would go to Burbank. They didn't have a simulator, it was more of a cockpit procedure trainer, a cockpit mock-up.

Jim: How often did you fly?

Steve: Again, that varied. When I started, we didn't have any aircraft. When I left, we had twenty-six or twenty-seven aircraft so we had a whole squadron of guys and we were flying the F-117A about three times a week, I guess, and the A-7 a couple of more times a week.

Ground crews perform post flight checks of the landing gear and install the gear locking pins in the Nellis Arm/Disarm area on F-117A 814. Once cleared, the aircraft would then taxi in to the ramp area. Visible are the twin retractable ILS antennas located just behind the cockpit. Additionally, the FLIR is in the view position. (Author)

Jim: In essence, did you fly every day?

Steve: You only had four flying nights a week - Monday through Thursday - because Friday you went home. It cut down on your normal flying time. A normal squadron would have five days of flying. You flew two out of four of those nights - average about three.

Jim: Was it two F-117A flights to one A-7 flight?

Steve: You got about three F-117A flights. We were shooting for ten to twelve a month. Getting about ten-twelve a month after we had over twenty aircraft. Then, you would get another five-six A-7 flights a month at least.

Jim: After the collective briefing, you went to individual threat assessment. Most missions were training, but were they designed to demonstrate and evaluate different operational missions, different scenarios that you may run into?

Steve: Yes, we used different areas of the world as a threat simulator that night. They had all kinds of computer technology, a lot of fancy stuff that I cannot go into, to do a lot of the mission planning and a lot of the real life threat assessment. It was really high tech and we used a lot of that for the regular missions.

Jim: When you went in for your initial briefing through the flight, what kind of time of day were you looking at?

Steve: We worked twelve hours a day. If we went in at 1 pm, you might get out of there between midnight and 0300. That is in the winter. In the summer, a mission planner might go in at 1500 and the rest of the guys would have to go in at 1700 to 1800. Normally, in the summer, we didn't get out of there until 0300 or 0400, sometimes 0500 - a lot of times I saw the sun come up. It was almost always a twelve hour night, that is when you would go back. They had an officer's club for us. We would have a couple of drinks then head to bed and probably sleep maybe six-seven

hours because it is the middle of the day. Then you got up and went to play tennis or something. The hard part was, you came home Friday and you were with your family and kids and you had a normal day Friday, Saturday and Sunday, then Monday we would generally only fly one mission and try to be done by midnight so it wouldn't be too bad. Tuesday, Wednesday and Thursday, however, you were up until anywhere from 0100-0600. You had to change your time clock eight to nine hours every week. You got used to it, but you got a little more tired as the week went on, then catch up on the weekend. Then, Monday wasn't too bad but by Thursday morning, you were a wreck.

Jim: Were most of the training missions over the West Coast?

Steve: Yes.

Jim: Did you venture anywhere else?

Steve: No, all the real training missions were out West. We did some test missions in different areas but the actual mass training missions were all out West.

An F-117A pulls off a KC-135Q tanker on 19 August 1990 as the F-117As of the 415th Tactical Fighter Squadron deployed to Saudi Arabia as part of Operation DESERT SHIELD. The aircraft flew non-stop from Langley, Virginia to Saudi Arabia. (Mike Dornheim)

An F-117A approaches a tanker to refuel with the rotating refueling port open. The FLIR turret is rotated forward revealing the wide field of view infrared TV camera (center) and to the left are the lens openings for the narrow field of view camera and the laser designator. (Mike Dornheim)

Jim: I have to assume that every training mission incorporated one or more in-flight refueling.

Steve: No, you normally refueled once a week, which is a lot. Normal Air Force requirements is three times a half, i.e. once every two months. We did it once a week. That wasn't just for our training, but also for the Boomers, the KC-10s and KC-135s because those were special crews who had to be briefed into the program.

Jim: Did they have a difficult time refueling the black airplane?

Steve: Yes, because it was all done lights out and no talking.

Jim: Without lights, how could they find...?

Steve: When you opened the fuel door, there is a little light there. The tankers would turn off everything but the top rotating beacon and one of the small lights on the bottom. They turned their inboard lights way down. They were just kind of a dim outline, we were basically nothing at all. That's why they had to have a lot of training for the Boomers because it was hard for them.

Jim: Did the Boomer have an idea what he was refueling?

Steve: Yes, depending on the how early in the night and the moon. When there was a moon you could see everything, especially over the snow it was like on a cloudless day. On a moonless night it was tough; they couldn't see us on a moonless night.

Jim: Without communications between the F-117A and the tanker, how could they get into the correct position?

Steve: We had certain times, and that was part of the briefing on tanker nights, when he would leave his IP and we would leave our point at a certain time and be coming toward each other. We had air to air tack ends. If that didn't work, you used timing. He would start a turn when he was supposed to. We would pick him up visually or through our systems, and rejoin on him in the turn, just like a normal refueling where he turns and you roll out a mile behind him, pull up there, open your door and when he sees you, he plugs you.

Jim: I was a refueling operator way back when on KC-97s in 1962. There was a lot of chatter between the Boomer and the pilot.

Steve: Well, there is a lot more than you need, but that is normal Air Force technique. The way we did it was, of course, radio out because we would have had to do it on a covert mission somewhere. You can't be talking. The guy who has the flight plan is the KC-10, and you are sitting there with him or are somewhere off and will meet him.

Jim: When I was at Beale, I saw an area marked off just north of Tonapah that was marked A28 or B26 special. Was that the refueling place? It was a teardrop shape.

Steve: That was a regular refueling track, it wasn't anything special. But most of the time we refueled on the range. We just built our own track on the range. We refueled over range air space.

Jim: In case something happened and you ever had to leave the airplane and it crashed, it would be on the range.

Steve: Yes, in fact, for the first year or so we never flew off range, they made us stay on range until they knew it had enough reliability to go off range without having a fair chance of dropping one somewhere.

Jim: Was the reliability pretty good?

Steve: Excellent. Well above expectations.

Jim: When you were going through your training flights and simulated missions, did you do high, low, or mixed profiles?

Steve: Yes, everything.

Jim: Once you acquired a target, how long did you track it before simulated weapons released? I have to assume that on the range sometimes you dropped live weapons.

Steve: Yes, we had to only track it precisely while the bomb was in the air for the time of fall of the weapon. That is all you have to track. Actually, you don't have to track it that precisely until 8-10 seconds of the flight time of the weapon. Then, you have to be precise because that is when it is guided.

Jim: On the DLIR, was there a laser illuminator? It looks like there are two other devices, a round one and two other circular ones next to it. How did you illuminate the target?

Steve: Again, this stuff was all internal, nothing hanging out.

Jim: Did you illuminate the target from the DLIR?

Steve: Either or.

Jim: The FLIR was steerable. Was the DLIR also steerable?

Steve: Sure.

Jim: When you are operating against simulated or assumed offenses, does the aircraft have radar homing or warning receivers to know that you have been illuminated?

Steve: I don't think they ever made a aircraft without a RAW. It does have one, yes.

Jim: Does it tell you from what direction it is coming?

Steve: No, it was a state of the art one at the time.

Jim: Because you operated almost without any communications during your simulated and covert missions, does the absence of communication lead to stress or make your job any more difficult?

Steve: No. It is great - nice and quiet.

Jim: How do you monitor other traffic?

Steve: On the range we did routes sometimes, most of the time we never went without the antennas out so you could still hear people talking and you could talk too. It wasn't that we never did communicate. On the range, we didn't need to because it was set up that way. When we went off range, we talked with center just like a normal A-7 would. They just thought we were A-7s flying at night.

Jim: Did you have an A-7 type transponder?

Steve: Yes, they are all the same.

This once in a lifetime opportunity occurred on 1 April 1991, when the 37th TFW had its homecoming from DESERT STORM at Nellis AFB, Nevada. Seven of the eight returning F-117As are visible. The aircraft are 830, 810, 814, 808, 825, 791 and 843. (Author)

Jim: So, you would turn that system on and they would see an A-7 and think they were talking to an A-7?

Steve: Yes.

Jim: I assume that you fly mainly by instruments at night.

Steve: Yes.

Jim: Were the systems really reliable?

Steve: Yes, I would say they were real reliable, although we did have problems with sometimes aligning precisely where your lasers were going with where you are looking. For the most part, the aircraft was real reliable and the systems were real good. Even though some of them were brand new systems, the reliability was great.

Jim: What did you do in case of a failure?

Steve: We had backups. There were regular gauges, pneumatic gauges.

Jim: So, if you lost your IR system.

Steve: No, you are talking parts of the weapons system now, but if you lose a certain aspect of your weapons system it is like any airplane. In an F-15 if you lose certain parts of the radar, you can not fire an AIM-7. So if you lose certain parts of your weapons system, you might as well turn around and go home. You can drop a bomb, but it is not going to be a smart bomb.

Jim: Does the F-117A have the same weapons bay capacity as an F-111?

Steve: No, nowhere near - the F-111 is a lot bigger airplane. I don't know how big the F-111 weapons bay is, but it is a much bigger airplane with a much bigger bay. No, I won't say it has a much bigger bay, because I don't know what the F-111 bay is like, but I am assuming it is bigger just because the airplane is so much bigger.

Jim: On the sensor turret with the FLIR and the DLIR, it looks as if there are three optical aptitudes. The hypothesis I have is one is wide field, one is narrow field - telephoto targeting. Is the other one laser?

Steve: Those are pretty good guesses.

Jim: Concerning the attack sequence, once the INS has brought you into the general vicinity of the target, what do you do from there?

Steve: Do you know anything about IR systems? They give you a good picture but you still have to identify the target. It might be a certain building in a big city. Now you have to identify it using heat radiation so it doesn't look exactly like a building maybe. Just looking at a photograph of a city where a building is circled as a target - it may or may not look like that through the IR display, depending on whether there is fresh snow on the ground and it is all the same temperature. There could be a lot of change, so target study is a real big player. The best to pick up is something like empty fields. There is a field of trees over there that is always going to be a cold spot no matter if it snows or rains, or if there has been sun all day or not. You will always be able to see that. Maybe it is three blocks this way and two blocks that way and it is the building on the corner from there. You need to pick out some prominent features and do some real good target study because you don't have a long time to see this thing. It also depends on the weather that night as to how far out you will be able to see the target. It could be anywhere from seconds to maybe minutes.

Jim: Was there a typical altitude at which you came in?

Steve: That would depend on the threat.

Jim: The lower you were, the less time you had to acquire the target?

Steve: Definitely, it would also look much different the lower you were.

Jim: What went through prior to going on the simulated run? Did RF-4s go through and photograph it or U-2s, or satellites? I am assuming that you had to have imagery.

Steve: Yes, we used all of them in various phases to get our imagery and the stuff on the range. We went out and took pictures ourselves from the air when we first started.

Jim: Would it be possible in an area where current coverage wasn't available or satellite wasn't acceptable, could you fly a F-117A in a couple of days before to do a scan of the area?

Steve: No, there would be some kind of imagery available. Whether it was good or not wouldn't matter too much, depending on the target. If it was a hard target such as a hardened underground bunker with a smoke stake sticking up for heat loss or breathing in the middle of a forest and that is all there is, you are going to have to have an accurate picture of exactly where it is. You are not going to be able to find it any other way. If it is a building - the Sears in downtown Chicago, you may not need a picture. You can probably pick that out. It depends on the target.

Jim: When you are getting ready to put your evening flying together and you were on your pre-brief, were you part of the mission planning as far as preparing the information for the mission tapes?

Steve: We took turns so everybody got a chance to do it.

Jim: Is that a very complex task?

Steve: Yes, it can be, depending on how complex the mission is. After we had been doing this a year or so, we had a lot of approved routes. All of our off-range routes had to be approved by the guys in the White House, so we had certain routes that went off-range. We could hit targets anywhere we wanted, but routes were approved so that you couldn't go make up a route off-range.

A pair of F-117As parked in front of the control tower at Tonopah Test Range. The aircraft in the foreground is Number 832, the forty-eighth production aircraft (delivered 11 February 1988) while the aircraft in the background is Number 793, the ninth production aircraft. (Eric Schulzinger)

You could though, on-range. If you wanted to do that, it would take a lot more mission planning. It just depended on what you wanted to do that night as the mission planner, and what the objective for the night was as to how long your mission planning might take. It might take an hour; it might take 3 or 4 hours.

Jim: You only had two weapons. On a night time mission with refueling involved, would you have more than two simulated targets? Would you go through half a dozen, a dozen?

Steve: Target wise, it would depend. Normally, you would have two simulated targets and a lot of turn points which you would have to find. You would have to find all the turn points and the targets and identify them. That was part of your grading criteria.

Jim Was there some taping system, video taping?

Steve: Yes. Other nights we had like a turkey shoot. We would go out and they would give you a route and fourteen turn points, which were in reality fourteen targets - real hard things - and you had to find each one and you got points for each one. That was how you determined the winner for the night.

Jim: What would be the most difficult target that you had to acquire?

Steve: The hardest stuff was cold things. Buildings, any kind, where people lived and there was heat you could find. You might mis-identify them in a big city just because it may not have been readily visible, but the hardest things were man made structures like a fire warden's little shack on a mountain in the trees. There wasn't much heat coming out of that thing and it might be covered with snow and it is not exactly on top of the mountain although the map shows a little symbol sitting on the top of a hill. How close of coordinates could you get? You might get within a mile of it, now you have to search that area trying to find the cold object in the middle of the woods. A dirt road intersection is real tough if it had just snowed. Situations where there was not much ambient heat or not much difference in the background radiation was real hard to detect. You could say they were unrealistic targets. Some of them were, but other ones could have been to find an underground bunker underneath that, so you would have to identify it. Buildings and normal bridges, normal targets were fairly easy.

Jim: You mentioned when we last spoke, that there were two occasions where you were pretty close to launching on a real mission. How many aircraft were you looking at to get ready to go.

Steve: We are not going to talk about that stuff yet.

Jim: The authority to launch, did that come from the Secretary of Defense, or the President?

Steve: That would have come through the President, not directly to us, but through him to either Weinberger to us or from Weinberger to perhaps the Tac DO at the time, whoever that was. There were a few of them since we were there. I am not sure the exact chain of command it would have followed down, but it would have come from the President.

COL Al Whitley's F-117A (813) on the ramp at Nellis AFB for the homecoming of the 37th TFW after DESERT STORM. The aircraft carries twenty-nine mission markings in Light Gray under the cockpit. This was the first public display of an F-117A with the weapons bay door open. (Author)

Jim: The entire operation was to be flown from Tonapah to the location. Were you going to return to Tonapah or recover somewhere else?

Steve: I don't want to go into that either. We will wait. Once they come out with some more stuff on that -it may be a few years - I will go into more detail. Eventually, it will come out.

Jim: Did you ever have any encounters where on a nighttime mission in the San Joaquim Valley that you came close to or encountered civilian or commercial aircraft? Or did you go out of your way to avoid that?

Steve: We did both. We went out of our way to avoid it, plus we wouldn't go off-range over big cities like that ever because of the background lighting from the big city. Under certain circumstances, like a high overcast, you don't want to be flying under it. If there is more than 50% moon, we didn't go on a lot of routes because of that. The amount of moon out dictated where we went. That was mainly it, how big the lighting of the city was and the moonlight. On a bright night, you could see that thing like in daytime especially with snow on the ground, so we stayed on range.

Jim: When John Andrews from Testors and I were there in September, what amazed me was that when the aircraft took off - and they took off in 5 to 8 minute intervals - to the south, then they turned to the east and started heading northwest. Every single aircraft, every time I have been there, the aircraft seemed to head toward the northwest. Is there a particular route there - are they heading towards Falon?

Steve: *That is the standard instrument departure - SID - just like any other place you fly out of. It goes to Tonapah first, where the airport is. That is the way they turn, which is 17 miles away, that is your first point. You are on an IFR flight plan just like any other plane and you take off and head over there, then to the rest of the points. That is why they always go there.*

Jim: It seems like they go out 10-15 miles from the end of the runway when they are heading south from the Tonapah area.

Steve: *Again, that is just your IFR approach and they are intersecting the arc down there, a 12 or 15 mile mark to line up on the IOS final. Evidently, they are still doing that and I don't know if they will ever shoot regular overhead patterns just because - we do regular instrument patterns.*

Jim: On a nighttime operation, from the time you got up, would you go through your entire day - mission planning, loading tapes, checking weapons?

Steve: *Again, we will pick a summer day since it is longer than winter. On a normal day, I would probably get up about noon, go out and run. They had a gym which a lot of guys used; I didn't. Then go eat lunch with a couple of guys. I would go back, and in the summer, I would normally play tennis with one of the guys. Then back to the room to shower, clean up and change, maybe eat supper, depending on the schedule. If I was mission planner that day, I would go in at 4 p.m. - get the bus out there, get it, take a look at the weather, all that stuff, pick some routes for that night, depending on the moonlight and weather conditions. If it is off range or on range, I had to pick routes and see how many planes were flying that night, to deconflict the routes. Let's say a route could handle 8 airplanes and we had 12 launching in the first goal. Then you had to pick 2 routes. Somewhere they were going to intersect or conflict, so now you had to deconflict the launch times and the times that airplanes are passing the points that conflict. The guys that will be passing those points will have to know that someone will be near them at that time. So mission planning may take a couple of hours which involve quite a bit of stuff. Then, getting the tapes ready for the routes among other things back there were the computers. The chow truck would show up between 5 and 6 p.m. It was like a traveling ice cream truck, but it had hot chow. You*

Ground crewmen pull the chocks from the main landing gear as the taxi director signals the pilot to hold his position. From below or directly to the rear, the engine exhaust ports are not visible. (Eric Schulzinger)

could go out to get a platefull of that and take it back in and eat, then get ready for the mass briefing. You, as mission planner, had to bring all the stuff to that; you would make copies of all the routes, turn points, targets, air speed heading and regular flight plans for each pilot, plus their tape to put in the plane.

Jim: Was the mission tape externally or internally mounted? I know on the SR-71 they loaded it externally from the bottom.

Steve: *No, it was all internal and you could punch it in yourself, too, If you got bad coordinates or if the tape was bad, you could do it all manually inside the airplane. The mass briefing would start at 1830 for a first takeoff at 2100. Everybody would get together after chow and set up the slides. I, as mass briefer, would brief the mission. Actually, it was like a regular Air Force briefing, but you are briefing everybody on the mission instead of one or two other people on the flight. You would start with a time hack, all the standard stuff, where a weatherman got up and told you how the weather was going to be along a route. Normally, he would go through a realistic weather brief from somewhere else in the world where we might be simulated to be going that night. Let's say that we were simulated to go to Tehran. He would go through the real weather brief for Tehran that night at that time. After the weather, all the basic stuff was out of the way, then you went through the mission itself, showing everybody the routes. Each guy would have a different launch time. It might be anywhere from 2 to 10 minutes apart. If you were going to hit a tanker, then the timing was a lot more critical because the guy has a launch time, and IP time, then a time to hit the tanker. If he missed the tanker, he would have to go through a different route because he might not have enough gas to fly that one. It could get to be a ball of wax on those nights.*

Jim: Were there times when they did miss the tanker?

Steve: *Oh yes, there were times guys would miss during your first few refuelings, but it could happen any time, whether the tanker was in the bad weather trying to get out of it and you were the first guy up on him and couldn't find him. Or, if it was a clear, dark night and he went into a cloud, you might not know it was there. Guys miss for various reasons. Sometimes, maybe a plane would abort and you could move up the flow 10 minutes because that guy was out of the picture. On certain nights, we did everything radio-out, including starting engines, taxiing and everything else, and you never even talked to ground or tower, so you had a certain time to start taxiing. Everything was on a time sequence. Anyway, getting back to the schedule, depending on the complexity of the mission, the mass briefing took between 20-40 minutes. On a real simple night, you could finish in 20 minutes, but normally 30-40 minutes. Then, the guys took their stuff and went back to look at their target and turn points so they could identify them, do their own mission planning (which would consist of going through their particular flight plan to make sure all the times were right with the mileages between points and the heading, and make sure everything looked right), then do a target study. Then, they would start going out to the airplanes. Launching 12 airplanes might take 2 hours if there were 10 minutes between them. As soon as the mass briefing was done, 20 minutes later the first guy might head out the door, but there were 2 hours before the last guy headed out. Things can get compressed for the first guy but not so much for the last guy. You would go get dressed, do the normal stuff on the way out, i.e., sign a log and everything just like a normal flight, head out to the airplane for preflight. The plane would already have power on it. Maintenance would have already gone over the plane and the INS was already aligning. They were great maintenance guys.*

Jim Could they put 2 aircraft in each hangar or just one.

Steve: *No, they do not put in two. The F-117A is a big aircraft, as you can see by the dimensions. The plane is running, you do your pre-flight standard and look over the aircraft, climb in and get ready to go. It doesn't take as long as a lot of aircraft, from the time you get to the aircraft. If you*

The last production F-117A on display at Air Force Plant 42, Lockheed Plant 10, Palmdale, California during the acceptance ceremony held on 12 July 1990. With the delivery of this aircraft, F-117A production came to a halt. (Tony Landis)

had to be started and gone in a couple of minutes, you could - if you were running late or if you had to move up into someone else's spot — because, the plane is sitting there, with the power on and it is all warmed up. It is not running, but it has power on it, the INS is aligning. As long as the INS was finished aligning, you could start up and go. It does take a while for the INS to align. You could take a short alignment but you would get reduced accuracy, although on a normal night, we went with short alignments for a lot of different reasons. Normally, we went with short alignments on the second goal of the night, not the first. But normally, it was accurate enough, almost as accurate as a full alignment which was very accurate. So you would go out and do your pre-flight, climb in, start up on time and out you went. The first guy would normally start about,... I don't remember the exact time. He couldn't open the doors on the hangars until official twilight. We had charts that told us official twilight. We didn't have sensors, we had a yearly thing that showed moonrise and sunset and moonrise tables that showed when it was official in Tonapah. It was made for Tonapah, for the altitude up there. I don't remember when official twilight was anymore, it is something like 1/2 hour after sunset. Anyway, you could not open the doors until then so that dictated the first launch of the night. So, the doors open, that guy starts up, taxies out and off he goes on his route. Again, the last guy might leave a couple of hours later. Normally, a standard flight mission lasted for an hour ten, an hour twenty, an hour thirty at the most.

Jim: So you didn't venture that far from home?

Steve: The longest routes might go a couple hundred, 250-300 miles at the most. I don't recall the farthest. You could go anywhere from 2-300 miles and back on just a normal flight. So you went out and got your flight plan from the tower, took off and now you were just an A-7 with a normal A-7 call sign if you were going off range. The first guy you talked to is at the center there. If you stayed on range, then you were talking to the Dreamland boys all night long and then we wouldn't talk too much. You got up and got a radio check in with them so they knew you were airborne and you knew they could hear you. Then we wouldn't say anything after that.

Jim: Did you generally retract the antennas?

Steve: No, not generally. There were a lot of nights when we did retract the antennas and I really don't remember....but with those retracted you couldn't talk to anybody or hear anybody so you had to remember to put them back out before you tried to talk. You never flew off range with the antennas up because nobody could talk to you and you couldn't hear anything. So you flew your mission, tried to identify all the target and turn points, did your simulated bomb drops or real bomb drops or BTUs - whatever you were carrying for the night.

Jim: Where did you drop your bombs?

Steve: On range. Everything off range, we never carried any weapons just so there wouldn't be any accidents.

Jim: On range means Nellis, or did you also go to China Lake?

Steve: We would go all over. China Lake, any of the Edwards ranges, Falon, Mountain Home and Utah UTR there. So anything within a couple of hundred miles was fair game after a year or so, when they started letting us off range. We had a lot of different ranges to go to so we had tons of different targets. You could always be looking at something different, so night after night you were not going after the same target that you could identify easily because you had been there a night ago. You were always looking at something different which made it real challenging. Target ID and turn point ID was good. On the turkey shoot nights where you might have 14 separate targets, some guys could get all of them. Some of them were real miniscule targets, such as a fire warden's tower in a forest or an intersection of a couple of dirt roads out in the middle of nowhere, or one of the hardest was finding a dock on the Marina at Lake Tahoe. That was a bitch, and I don't know if anyone did find that.

Jim: Was it a specific dock?

Steve: Yes, and it was hard enough to find the Marina on Lake Tahoe and then to find a dock. The water is so cold that it didn't show up at all - it was real tough. With normal targets, it was fairly simple. We had no qualms about using the system and going after any normal targets. That is why we picked hard things because the normal things were fairly easy. Anyway, so you would fly your mission - an hour and a half, come back and then fly a couple of instrument approaches until you burned down your gas load to normal flight fuel, about 2,000 pounds before you landed. As long as the weather was good, you would come back, shoot a couple of instrument approaches until you burned your gas down, or you wanted to land, or until it got to be too many people in the pattern and too congested. So, some would land - normally the first guy who got back.

Then, you were on the ground, you would go in and shut down. If it was going to turn for the second goal, they would hook up electrical power to keep the INS going and aircraft systems they wanted to keep going, or you could shut down and they could turn everything back on in a couple of hours, it didn't really matter. We did it both ways and it changed as we went, due to what Lockheed thought was the best way to do it. The way we did it in the beginning didn't necessarily turn out to be the best way later on, once we had done it a while. This again was because everything was new. Then you would go into debriefing first with the maintenance debriefers about any problem you had with the aircraft.

Jim: Were there any typical problems that you had?

Steve: No, there wasn't one thing more than any other. They were real, real good aircraft. A lot of the systems were off-the-shelf. You know, they were all new but off-the-shelf. Some of the stuff, like the flight control systems and some of the inards of the aircraft were built specifically, but a

An F-117A (830) lands at Nellis Air Force Base, Nevada on 1 April 1991. The aircraft was the 46th production aircraft and was delivered on 27 November 1987. The aircraft carries DESERT STORM mission markings under the canopy in Light Gray (port side only). (Author)

lot of the other things were right off-the-shelf and they just had to put it all together. There was real good reliability. Debrief, then get a ride up to the Ops building. If you were the first guy who launched and took off, let's say, at 9 p.m., you would land at 1030. You would get back into the building, say at 1105 p.m. or 1110 p.m. Then you would take off your boots and helmet, all that crap, and put it away. Then you would go look at your tape - your mission - to see if you did indeed identify everything. You might go look at it with a weapons guy or me, if I built the route that night. I would know what the targets were so I could look at them with you if you have any question like: "I'm not sure if this was really turn point six or if it was really this building over here - did I miss it." So, you would tell him whether it was right or wrong.

Jim: Are your turn points actual specific points?

Steve: Yes, it wouldn't have to be that specific, but we made them specific to give the guy something to do. He could simulate it being another target. In fact, we did a lot of simulated weapons drops on turn points because everyone you came up on, you could treat as a target and do a simulated weapons release without firing the laser, which you never did off-range. Never.

The Wing Commander's F-117A (813) was named _THE TOXIC AVENGER_ . This was the 29th aircraft and was delivered to the Air Force on 10 July 1985. The object suspended from the pylon is a Travel Pod, for the pilot's personal effects. (Author)

THE TOXIC AVENGER

Col. Al Whitley
37 TFW
COMMANDER

Jim: What was the reason for never firing the laser off-range?

Steve: Just so you didn't hurt anything, so we never fired them off-range.

Jim: Is it a visible laser?

Steve: No, so you went and did all that and you could be done anywhere from 2300 to 2400 on a typical mission, where you are not doing anything but flying. If you were the briefer, you had to wait for the last guy to land which could be 1230 a.m. As the last guys are landing, the first guys were going out for the second goal. It might be a guy that flew the first or second mission on the first goal that might have another flight on the second goal of the night. Or it might be some other guys. The second goal might be going back out and starting their takeoff at midnight to 0100. There is an interchange there with some guys coming in and others going out. Basically, everybody debriefs themselves unless they have questions, or unless it is a special night, like a weapons comp, etc... Then a weapons guy would look at all the targets. He is the final decision making man as to whether or not you did identify the right target.

Let's say you were the number one guy on the first flight and you didn't have anything else to do, i.e., you weren't IPing for anybody that night, and you didn't have to grade sheets, etc. You then were basically done at midnight. What would you do? Well, you could go do some studying. We all had other jobs. I was chief of training and scheduling when I was there, besides being a flight commander. You might have to write OER's or do the schedule for the next day or the day after, or work on training. You did your normal daily activities at night which you would have done after a normal afternoon of flying. You did them at 0100 or 0200. You would do that until the second crew landed. The first guy took off at 2400, they would begin to land at 0130 until about 0300. We tried to have everybody on the ground between 0230 and 0300 in the winter. We would have to sometimes fly a little later than that in the summer. Normally, everybody would be down by about 0300. Then, when the debriefer did all his stuff, it was about 0400. Everybody would head home, probably head into the bar for a drink or two, or head to bed. Some guys would head to the chow hall to get breakfast. So we were done at 0400. The debriefer showed up at 1500 that afternoon. That was a thirteen hour night for him. For a normal guy who showed up at 1700, that was only eleven hours. The first flyer that night who got done at 2230 and done at midnight, probably did some paperwork and was able to go home at 2 a.m. It might only have been a 10-hour night for him. There wasn't any reason to go home early, because the bar was there and was

This F-117A (789) on the taxiway at Edwards Air Force Base, California was the fifth aircraft delivered to the USAF (17 November 1982). The aircraft carries the insignia of TAC and the 37th TFW on the fin. (Tony Landis)

open. All the day workers, officers who did CVPO and radio, etc. in the base were there until midnight, then they headed off to bed to be ready for their normal. If you got there between midnight and 0200, all the day-shift guys are gone and flyers weren't there yet. Most guys just waited around until everyone was done flying, then we headed home.

That was your typical day, it got pretty long.

Jim: Were there any times when you flew real long simulated missions?

Steve: Yes, we did endurance rides. They weren't for the pilots, it was to see how reliable the aircraft were.

Jim: Was that to simulate flying from here to Europe or the Middle East?

Steve: Yes, we did those time-length missions just right over the range.

Jim: When you talk about the "range," would that only be the Nellis range or would that be the entire complex encompassing Edwards, China Lake?

Steve: No, we could do that but normally we just did it over Nellis range. If you were going to do it for hours and hours, you would do it just over Nellis.

Jim: Wouldn't that get real boring?

Steve: Sure, but that is not for pilot proficiency, it is to test the equipment. So, when you are a test pilot, test pilot work is pretty boring.

Jim: What was the longest that any aircraft did?

Steve: We did a long time - I don't want to tell you exactly. But pick anywhere in the world and we would fly it. From here to Europe is at least 8 hours from the east coast. You could figure that we did at least something that long because that is a pretty prime place to go.

Jim: If you were to simulate or actually fly to the Far East, operate out of Osan, would you go midway and stop at Johnson Island which is a real secure facility?

Steve: We would stop somewhere on that route just because it was too darn long for the pilot. It was something like 17 hours, which is too darn long. Whether it would be one of those or going into Hawaii at night with a couple of aircraft and throwing them into hangars with guards around them and then taking off the next night - you could do that on a dark night. Actually, that is just speculation. We would do something like that, yes.

Jim: I understand that there were half a dozen or so bases that if you got into an emergency situation, that you already had pre-approval.

Steve: What it started out with was as soon as we started flying off-range we knew that if we had an emergency, we might have to go into some of these other places if we couldn't make it back. Initially, they gave us a letter from - I can't remember who signed it now, let's just say it was - a TACDO, a 2 or 3-star general. Anyway, it was from somebody pretty high. It said "Dear Wing Commander or Base Commander," basically it said, "Do what this guy says and call me in the morning." Signed, umpty umpt. So, if you ever had to go in anywhere, you would land and call ground to open a hangar, then shut down and get some guards out. Then the Wing Commander shows up and you tell him that you want everybody that was in on this - everybody that I talked to and everybody that was out here to see me in here now - to get debriefed and to sign a statement that says that they won't say anything about this ever.

That is how it started out. Then, they went to the prime bases around there and talked to, I guess it would be, the Wing Commander and said if anything unusual ever lands here and a guy with a piece of paper shows up, do what he said. They never told them anything, but said he might have something unusual come in one night and to please do what the pilot said.

Then, again, a few years later down the road, we had actual things set up. At Nellis, for one, there was a designated hangar in one of the hush houses down at the end of the runway - I don't know what they store in there, it was just a hangar at the end of the runway that they actually did practically—

The ground crew buttons up this F-117A as it is prepared for its first ever public static display. The aircraft has been roped off to keep the crowds at a proper distance. The coiled wire running from the wheel well to the ramp is a static ground wire. (Author)

This was the first time I ever saw an F-117A, 1415 hours on 24 August 1989 at the northern fence line of the Tonopah Test Range. The fact that the aircraft is accompanied by a T-38A chase plane, indicates that it is being flown by a new pilot under training. (Author)

tices - with an A-7, not an F-117A. An A-7 lands and they throw a tarp over it and haul it in there real quick. They were ready for that stuff once we started flying off range. Now, if something had happened the first time we flew off range, it would have been a goat-rope and we probably would never have gone off range again until they got it straightened out. Luckily, nothing ever did.

Jim: Did you ever have an engine failure? And if so, how does it react?

Steve: *We never had an engine that failed that I recall. We had false engine fire, maybe, an indication on the engine that there was a fire when there really wasn't. We had some other problems where you might shut down an engine, something like low oil pressure, so you shut it down, but there was no problem flying with a single engine. The aircraft operates real good. It is basically center line thrust. You don't get too much yaw or anything. It is not hard to fly at all. It has enough power.*

Jim: Considering the F-117A as an operational aircraft, and it has been operational for a number of years of flying, why is it that they still fly with a chase? Is it because they can track the chase?

Steve: *No, what they are doing over there with chase now is training, from what I assume, because that is what we always used to do for training. You got a new guy in a new aircraft, and he is checking out and he can't put an IP in his back seat so they put him in the aircraft next to him. So when you see chasing, it is training going on. That is, the IP in the chase aircraft talking to a new guy in the aircraft.*

It may even be, not necessarily a new guy. I don't know how that they work it during the daytime now. Sometimes they chase, just to chase in the daytime when they can. At night, it is not feasible to do. 90% of what you are seeing out there is training.

Jim: 90% of the flights that I have seen and for a person that is not part of the program, I have seen a lot of F-117A launches and with the exception of the evening of the 13th of September when the 17 aircraft took off as individual aircraft without chase, there is always a T-38. During the daytime, the T-38 takes off first. He does a race track, goes around the mountain, picks him up.

Steve *Yeah.*

Jim: As he makes his turn and is coming parallel to the runway, the F-117A takes off. As he climbs out, the T-38 comes in at his six then moves into his eight o'clock position.

Steve: *That's just an IP chasing a student.*

Jim: It seems that as they take off to the south, they always head to the east. Is that a typical turn point?

Steve: *No, that is just to stay in the range. When you go to the west, you are not going to get out of the range unless you really turn wide, but it is right on the edge of the air space. So, they turn east to stay on the range.*

Jim: When you are doing a simulated weapons launch, is there a throttle position you put it in to quiet it down. That is a noisy aircraft.

Steve: *No, normally you are going to be not high, because it depends on defenses and what you are trying to attack, but you don't really care too much about noise at the target. If they haven't picked you up by then, they will know something was around in just a few seconds anyway so you are not really concerned about noise. We don't do anything with the throttles for noise abatement.*

An F-117A on final approach to Tonopah followed by a T-38A chase aircraft. Chase aircraft are used during training missions of new pilots, since there are no two seat F-117As. The instructor flies in the T-38 and talks the new F-117A pilot through the mission. (Tony Landis)

Jim: Do you wear a standard flight suit and a partial G-suit?

Steve: Yes, same as any other aircraft.

Jim: From what I understand, they have three squadrons: the 415th, the 416th tactical fighter squadron and the 417th tactical fighter training squadron.

Steve: Oh! Well, that would be right.

Jim: Somewhere, in a recent publication, it said that they were operating fifty-three aircraft. That means they probably included the training aircraft and a couple of pre-production aircraft used in training.

Steve: Well, they lost a couple.

Jim: They lost three.

Steve: Maintenance always has one for maintenance training. Then there are always a couple being worked on - upgrading the older ones with the new systems, etc...

Jim: Was Palmdale the depot, when you were there?

Steve: Yes, it was, but they did a lot of the stuff right at Tonapah. They did major stuff there because it was easier than taking them back to Palmdale.

An F-117A (807) Stealth fighter is chocked on the ramp at the Tonopah Test Range, Nevada while another takes off on a rare daytime training mission. Most F-117A missions are flown at night. (Eric Schulzinger)

An F-117A Stealth fighter and the next Lockheed Stealth fighter — the YF-22 Advanced Tactical Fighter (ATF) prototype on the ramp at Air Force Plant 42, Palmdale, California. The YF-22 is Lockheed's (teamed with General Dynamics and Boeing)entry in the fly-off program against the Northrop/McDonnell-Douglas YF-23. (Eric Schulzinger)

F-117A Into Combat

On 28 October 1983, the 4450th Tactical Group was declared operational at the Tonopah Test Range Facility. This date is significant because the F-117A's first operational mission was considered before the aircraft was declared operational.

During October of 1983, the U.S. government ordered the Department of Defense to plan an attack on the PLO and PLO sympathizers/terrorists in southern Lebanon in response to the destruction of the Marine barracks in Lebanon. The Seventh Fleet in the Mediterranean was moved into position off the coast of Lebanon and the 4450th at Tonopah was put on alert. Five to seven aircraft were armed and their INS systems aligned to targets in the area.

The plan called for the F-117As to fly from Tonopah to Myrtle Beach, South Carolina, where they would be put into hangars. They would wait 48 hours for crew rest and then fly the aircraft non-stop from Myrtle Beach to southern Lebanon. The attack was planned against positively identified locations of the terrorist groups that were known to be responsible for the deaths of 183 Marines of the peace keeping force in Beirut.

Casper Weinberger, the Secretary of Defense, decided to scrub the mission just forty-five minutes before the aircraft were to take off for Myrtle Beach. The F-117As were taken off alert, disarmed and had their INS systems reprogramed for training purposes.

By 28 February 1986, Lockheed had delivered thirty-three F-117As, giving the Air Force two squadrons of operational F-117As. During this time, Libya's COL Gaddafi had been waving his saber at the United States Navy for approximately a year and a half and had also sponsored a number of terrorist activities in Europe. After a few aerial incidents which resulted in the loss of a number of Libyan aircraft, and a terrorist attack in Germany that was positively linked by the United States to Libya, the U.S. government decided to strike back.

On 15 April 1986 a bombing raid on Libya was planned under the code name Operation EL DORADO CANYON. The F-117A was identified as the weapons system best suited for the mission. Although senior officers at TAC knew of the F-117A's capabilities, the theater commanders knew nothing of its capabilities or even that it existed. As a result, the raid was carried out using carrier based Navy A-6s, A-7s, F/A-18s, and USAF F-111s based out of the United Kingdom.

Once again, the F-117As were within less than one hour from launch when Casper Weinberger scrubbed the mission. He felt that the aircraft was too valuable to risk on such insignificant targets and the F-117A's participation in the raid was therefore cancelled.

Finally on the night of 19 December 1989, the F-117A flew its first combat mission. GEN Manuel Noriega had become an embarrassment to the United States and a threat to the health and well-being of Panama. It was decided that a military invasion of Panama would be undertaken to remove Manuel Noriega from power under the name Operation JUST CAUSE. On the night of 19 December 1989, six F-117As took off from Tonopah and joined with two KC-10A tankers for the flight from Tonopah to Brownsville, Texas. From Texas, they flew directly across the Caribbean to Panama. Total mission flying time from Tonopah to Panama was approximately six and a half to seven hours with a number of aerial refuelings enroute to the targets.

There were six mission aircraft. Two were backup aircraft, with two aircraft assigned to each of the the two primary targets. Just prior to entering Panamian airspace, one of the targets was scratched. The two aircraft that had been designated for this target turned and headed back to Tonopah. The two remaining F-117As were given geographic coor-

An F-117A on the ramp at Nellis Air Force Base, Nevada for the change of command ceremony of the 37th TFW. COL Alton Whitley relieved COL Tony Tolin as commander, just two days before the unit deployed twenty F-117As to Saudi Arabia. (Marty Isham)

dinates of their targets by the Army (not landmarks). They dropped two (of four) 2,000 pound laser-guided Paveway II bombs, with one hitting the target and the other reportedly hitting several thousand yards from its designated target. It is believed that the F-117A pilot bombed the coordinates he was given (which were in error).

It was Saddam Hussein, the President and dictator of Iraq, who set into motion events that allowed the F-117A to finally prove its worth as a first line tactical strike bomber.

On 2 August 1990, Saddam Hussein ordered the Iraqi army to invade the country of Kuwait. In response, the United States, at the request of Saudi Arabia, began Operation DESERT SHIELD, a massive infusion of United States military men and equipment

An F-117A on final approach to landing at Langley Air Force Base, Virginia home of the 1st TFW on 19 August 1990. The aircraft remained overnight, then departed for Saudi Arabia the following day. (USAF)

into Saudi Arabia to prevent an Iraqi invasion. Intelligence information revealed that if the United States had not acted, Saddam, once he had secured Kuwait, would have moved against Saudi Arabia, the United Arab Emirates, Oman, Bahrain, and the rest of the Arabian peninsula. If successful, he would then have controlled some 50% of the oil in the free world, which was totally unacceptable to the U.S. and other western governments.

The F-117A Stealth fighter had been designed to respond to actions such as the invasion of Kuwait. The F-117A is a covert operations aircraft, designed for surgical strike against hardened, high-value, highly defended tactical/strategic targets. The aircraft was a weapons system capable of delivering a 2,000 pound laser-guided weapon from 25,000 feet under the cover of total darkness and hitting a one meter target. With this type of capability, the Air Force could quickly deliver a crippling blow against the Iraqi Armed Force's command and control system, making the air war against Iraq easier for more conventional strike aircraft.

On 19 August 1990, twenty-two F-117As of the 415th TFS, accompanied by about a dozen KC-135Qs from Beale Air Force Base, California flew to Langley Air Force Base, Virginia. They spent the night, and the following afternoon twenty of the F-117As departed Langley for the fifteen hour non-stop flight to Saudi Arabia. Enroute refueling was provided by Air Force/McDonnell Douglas KC-10A tankers. The two remaining F-117A spares were returned to Tonopah since they were not needed to make the overseas flight.

The aircraft arrived at a classified location within Saudi Arabia (reportedly a new Air Force Base that was not yet occupied). It appears from released photographs of the operating site that the base and the facilities were designed specifically for F-117A operations. Two aircraft were housed in each shelter, with purified filtered air and blast doors. The revetments, taxiways and parking aprons were all below ground level. The barracks and the housing facilities were air-conditioned, housing about twenty-two people. The base has a swimming pool, but its location is very isolated.

Ben Rich stated (when asked how the F-117As were fairing in Saudi Arabia) in a very delightful voice, "They are operating as expected. There have been no maintenance pro-

blems to speak of, and the environment and location they are operating out of is identical in terrain, altitude, and makeup to Tonopah. The aircraft are operating like a dream."

By mid-November 1990, it became obvious that Hussein was not going to pull out of Kuwait. President Bush made the decision to increase the number of troops within the theater from approximately 150,000 to nearly 450,000 combat and support troops. There were now approximately twenty-five hundred combat and support aircraft in the Gulf area from the countries of the coalition forces.

As part of this build up, a second operational squadron of F-117As deployed from Tonopah to Saudi Arabia. The 416th TFS was called up during mid-November to reinforce the twenty aircraft in country with a number of additional aircraft. By Thanksgiving Day the USAF had some forty F-117As in Saudi Arabia. With this force, the planners had the capability to attack targets within Iraq or Kuwait with eighty, 2,000 pound laser guided Paveway II or III bombs simultaneously, without the Iraqi Air Force or Air Defense System ever knowing the aircraft were in the area, much less intercepting them.

On 16 January 1991, Operation DESERT SHIELD became Operation DESERT STORM with the largest aerial bombardment in the history of modern warfare. During the first night of bombing against targets in Iraq and Kuwait, there were well over 1,000 sorties. That is equal to all the sorties flown during the invasion of Normandy on D-Day. The first manned USAF aircraft to fly into hostile Iraqi airspace were the F-117As of the 37th Tactical Fighter Wing.

At approximately 0130 on 17 January, two squadrons of F-117As dropped approximately sixty, 2,000 pound bombs on key Iraqi air defense, command and control facilities, ammunition bunkers, SCUD surface-to-surface missile bunkers, missile storage facilities, and the headquarters of the Iraqi Air Force. On 20 January 1991, GEN Schwarzkopf, Commander of U.S./Allied forces in the Gulf revealed to the media infrared video taken from an F-117A as it struck key targets within Iraq. One of the key targets that showed the capability of the F-117A was a view of a SCUD storage facility that had three air ducts on its roof, each approximately a meter in diameter. The main air duct was identified by the F-117A pilot and the laser cursor was locked on the center of the air duct. A 2,000 pound

The last of twenty-two F-117As of the 415th Tactical Fighter Squadron that deployed to Saudi Arabia on 19 August 1990 lands at Langley AFB, Virginia, for crew rest. Twenty aircraft departed Langley AFB, Virginia for Saudi Arabia with the two spares returning to Tonopah the next day. (USAF)

An F-117A lands at Langley Air Force Base, Virginia and rolls past six others that had landed earlier. A total of twenty-two F-117As made the flight from Tonapah, Nevada to Langley. The next day twenty aircraft continued on to the Middle East. (USAF)

An F-117A Stealth fighter moves into position for refueling from a SAC KC-135Q tanker during the squadron's non-stop flight from Langley, Virginia to the Middle East. (Mike Dornheim)

An F-117A Stealth fighter takes on fuel from a 22nd ARW KC-10A Extender over the Atlantic enroute to the Middle East. Each KC-10 led a flight of three/four F-117As. The aircraft carried the unit badge on the fuselage side in Gray. (USAF)

An F-117A moves up into position to take on fuel from a KC-10A tanker of the 22nd Air Refueling Wing, over the Atlantic enroute to the Middle East. The KC-10s provided refueling escort for the twenty aircraft that made the first deployment. (USAF/Combat Camera)

An F-117A of the 415th TFS, 37th TFW over the Atlantic Ocean enroute to Saudi Arabia on 19 August 1990. The aircraft did not carry the 37th TFW markings, TR tail code and TAC badge on the fin. For the ferry flight, all aircraft were equipped with removable rotating beacons. (Mike Dornheim).

laser-guided bomb was released and entered the bunker through the air duct. The SCUD storage bunker was totally destroyed in a spectacular explosion.

Another significant attack, shown on CNN and other major television networks, was an attack on an ammunition bunker near the city of Baghdad, Iraq. The F-117A illuminated the front door of the bunker and guided two 2,000 pound Paveway II LGBs into the target. The first blew down the door; the second one went inside and blew up the bunker. Again the F-117A pilot hit his target dead center.

The most impressive attack was, as revealed by GEN Kelly, Commander of Air Force Operations in DESERT STORM, an attack against, "My counterpart's headquarters in downtown Baghdad." The tape showed a square ten story building. In the center of the roof was an elevator shaft. The F-117A flew directly over the building, the laser cursor was locked on the elevator shaft and a BLU-109 deep penetration weapon was released. The weapon has a hardened steel casing capable of penetrating up to six feet of concrete and a delayed action fuse. It dropped through the top of the elevator shaft and appeared to go deep within the building before detonating. The video showed all four walls of the building being blown outward.

COL Al Whitley revealed that the F-117As flew some 1,271 sorties during the war, or about one per cent of the total sorties flown (110,000) by Allied Air Forces, with a success rate of 80%. The F-117As attacked thirty-one percent of all targets struck during the first twenty-four hours of the war, and were the only aircraft involved in attacks on heavily defended targets in and around Baghdad on the first night of the war. It was an F-117A that dropped the first bomb of the war, attacking a telecommunications center in Baghdad.

On the night of 16 January 1991, the F-117A proved beyond the shadow of a doubt that Ben Rich, of Lockheed's Advanced Development Projects, and his team of dedicated aerospace workers had built the most capable surgical strike aircraft in the history of modern warfare.

A pair of F-117As share an aircraft shelter in the Saudi Arabian desert. The aircraft remained in the shelters during the day and flew their missions after dark. (USAF via Knox Bishop)

COL Alton Whitley, Commander of the 37th TFW, led the unit into combat in Iraq when Operation DESERT SHIELD became Operation DESERT STORM on 16 January 1991. COL Whitley flew the first aircraft over Iraq that night and dropped the first GBU-27 I-2,000 pound bomb on the headquarters of the Iraqi Air Force. COL Whitley was one of the first USAF pilots to fly the F-117A during the test program. (USAF)

An F-117A (818) of the 415th TFS parked in a blast proof climate controlled shelter in Saudi Arabia. This aircraft was the thirty-fourth production aircraft delivered on 22 May 1986. (USAF via Knox Bishop)

An F-117A parked in a shelter in Saudi Arabia. These shelters, although not designed for the F-117A, proved to be well suited to F-117A operations. The Stealth crews named the location — Tonapah East. (USAF)

An F-117A parked in a revetted taxiway at a forward operating base in Saudi Arabia on 20 August 1990. The 37th TFW initially deployed twenty aircraft, followed by an additional twenty-two aircraft during November. (USAF/Combat Camera)

46

An F-117A Stealth fighter parked in a protected revetment in Saudi Arabia. After DESERT STORM began, some F-117As were seen carrying small White Paveway II laser-guided bomb markings under the cockpit to denote bombing missions against Iraqi targets. (USAF)

Three F-117As of the 37th TFW parked in a revetment in Saudi Arabia. The aircraft in the center is being fitted with the custom work/boarding ladder used with the F-117A while the aircraft in the background is using a commercially available folding ladder. The aircraft in the foreground was flown by a British RAF pilot. (USAF)

An F-117A of the 37th TFW on the ramp at Tonapah East, their operating base in Saudi Arabia. The trucks in the background are the support vehicles, delivered to the base by Lockheed C-5 transports within hours after the fighters arrived. (USAF)

F-117A Weapons

The primary weapon used on the F-117A is the GBU-10 Paveway II laser-guided bomb. This is a typical laser-guided weapon which consists of a special nose and tail section that is attached to a standard 2,000 pound Mk 84 bomb body. The tail section incorporates folding aerodynamic surfaces which allow the bomb to glide rather than to follow a standard ballistic path. The nose section includes a laser seeker, guidance electronics and control fins.

Another weapon carried by the F-117A is referred to as the BLU-109/B. During 1984, a DOD study showed that many targets in eastern Europe and elsewhere, were being hardened to the point that even a direct hit with a 2,000 pound bomb would leave them damaged but functional. Under the code name *Have Void*, an improved weapon was developed by the Lockheed Missile and Space Company. It was delivered during December of 1985 and is known as the I-2,000 (Improved 2,000 pound bomb) or BLU-109/B. The weapon is normally mated to a GBU-10 laser-guidance kit.

The BLU-109 is a slim, bullet shaped bomb with a tail fuse and a forged casing of hardened steel made in one piece, apart from the tail plug. In both rocket tests and live drop tests, BLU-109 warheads penetrated more than six feet of reinforced concrete and remained intact. The weapons then detonated reliably within the structure. The resulting explosion tossed 40 ton slabs of concrete all over the test range. Against softer targets, the weapon would bury itself deep before detonating, sending shock waves rippling through the ground (like an earthquake) and causing massive destruction. It is believed that a BLU-109 was the weapon used to destroy the Iraqi Air Force headquarters on 16 January 1991 during the initial bombing raid against Iraq at the beginning of Operation DESERT STORM.

The third weapon used is the laser-guided GBU-24 Paveway III, a more modern weapon with a larger tail surface and a more efficient navigation system. Apart from being essentially undetectable, this weapon is extremely accurate. Typically, a laser-guided weapon lands within feet of the point of illumination from the launching aircraft. It can be aimed with high confidence at any one of a cluster of small buildings, a window, a door, an elevator shaft — if they can see the target, they can hit it.

In April of 1990 when the F-117A was unveiled at Nellis Air Force Base, the Air Force stated that the F-117A can carry a full range of tactical munitions. Reportedly, this means that any weapon that can be carried in the weapons bay of an F-111 can be carried in the weapons bay of an F-117A (including the B-61 Tactical Nuclear Weapon). Like all Tactical Air Command aircraft, the F-117A is wired with a nuclear safeing system and is capable of delivering nuclear weapons. The F-117A, at this point in time, does not have a nuclear strike mission within TAC.

Air-to-air weapons are being considered and the weapons bay could easily accommodate two or four AMMRAM missiles on extendable launchers. The F-117A currently does not have an air-to-air mode and may never have an air-to-air capability, but the options are being looked at. There would have to be some modifications to the weapons bay to accommodate AMMRAMs, but the program is under study.

COL Al Whitley arrives at Nellis AFB on 1 April 1990 after a total of 220 days TDY in southwestern Saudi Arabia. The aircraft carries twenty-nine mission markings represented by GBU-27 bomb symbols under the cockpit. (Author)

Laser Guided Bombs

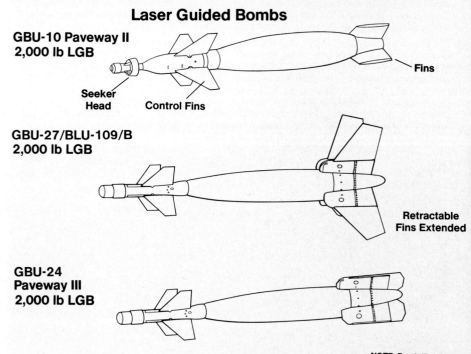

GBU-10 Paveway II
2,000 lb LGB

Seeker Head
Control Fins
Fins

GBU-27/BLU-109/B
2,000 lb LGB

Retractable Fins Extended

GBU-24 Paveway III
2,000 lb LGB

NOTE: Bomb Fins Are Separate Kits

48

The twin weapons bay doors on the underside of the fuselage are hinged to open along the aircraft centerline. Just forward of each weapons bay are two extended spoilers that reduce buffeting during weapons release. The weapons pylon is lowered into the airstream once the fast acting doors are fully opended. (Author)

This well houses the Downward Looking Infrared (DLIR) turret which is located on the starboard side of the nose wheel on the fuselage underside. The fastener heads are all covered with RAM putty. (Author)

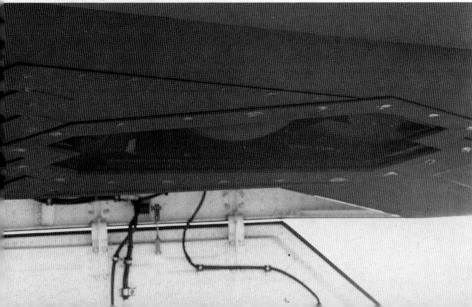

Weapons Bay Doors & Bomb Mount

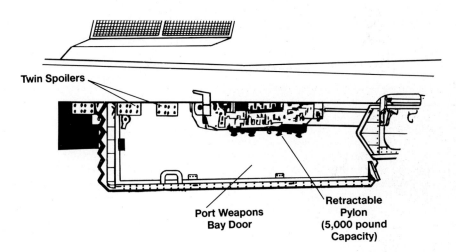

Twin Spoilers

Port Weapons Bay Door

Retractable Pylon (5,000 pound Capacity)

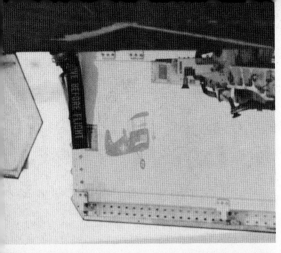

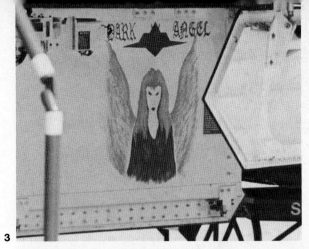

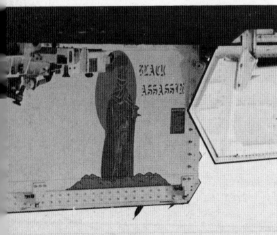

F-117A Nose Art

1. Aircraft 791 *LAZY ACE*
2. Aircraft 808 *THOR*
3. Aircraft 810 *DARK ANGEL*
4. Aircraft 813 *THE TOXIC AVENGER*
5. Aircraft 814 *FINAL VERDICT*
6. Aircraft 825 *MAD-MAX*
7. Aircraft 830 *BLACK ASSASSIN*
8. Mission Markings on *THE TOXIC AVENGER*